THE PORTFOLIO ORGANIZER

Succeeding with Portfolios in Your Classroom

Carol Rolheiser, Barbara Bower, and Laurie Stevahn

2000

ASCD

Association for Supervision and Curriculum Development
Alexandria, Virginia USA

Association for Supervision and Curriculum Development
1703 N. Beauregard St. • Alexandria, VA 22311-1714 USA
Telephone: 1-800-933-2723 or 703-578-9600 • Fax: 703-575-5400
Web site: http://www.ascd.org • E-mail: member@ascd.org

Gene R. Carter, *Executive Director*
Michelle Terry, *Deputy Executive Director, Program Development*
Nancy Modrak, *Director of Publishing*
John O'Neil, *Director of Acquisitions*
Joyce McLeod, *Developmental Editor*
Julie Houtz, *Managing Editor of Books*
Darcie Russell, *Associate Editor*
Gary Bloom, *Director, Design and Production Services*
Georgia McDonald, *Senior Designer*
W. Keith Demmons, *Graphic Designer*
Tracey A. Smith, *Production Manager*
Dina Murray Seamon, *Production Coordinator*

ASCD publications present a variety of viewpoints. The views expressed or implied in this book should not be interpreted as official positions of the Association.

This book contains authentic samples of work from teachers, students, and parents whenever possible. Permission to use these samples has been granted. To preserve authenticity and to present a realistic view of the work, the punctuation, spelling, and grammar has been preserved in the samples.

Printed in the United States of America.

s 6/2000

ASCD Product No. 100046
ASCD member price: $20.95   nonmember price: $24.95

Library of Congress Cataloging-in-Publication Data
Rolheiser-Bennett, Noreen Carol.
 The portfolio organizer : succeeding with portfolios in your classroom
/ Carol Rolheiser, Barbara Bower, and Laurie Stevahn.
    p. cm.
 Includes bibliographical references and index.
 "ASCD stock no. 100046"
 ISBN 0-87120-374-X
 1. Portfolios in education. I. Bower, Barbara, 1957- II. Stevahn,
Laurie, 1956- III. Title.
LB1029.P67R65 2000
371.2—dc21
                    00-008817

06 05 04 03 02 01 00   10 9 8 7 6 5 4 3 2 1

To Craig (Freebie),

You gave me the precious gifts of time, attention, support, and great meals when they were most needed. Your capacity for taking life seriously but never too seriously, and for tenaciously accepting the great mystery of life's laughter and tears, is remarkable. You are everything to me.

Carol

To Bill,

whose patience is endless and whose support has been unwavering. Your input into many facets of this work has been incalculable, because you have helped me to crystallize what it is that I truly believe in. Thank you for your love and encouragement.

Barb

To Steve, Ellen, and Mike,

my family, whose unconditional love provides the home base that gives profound meaning to my life's journey. Your wisdom, hope, fortitude, and grace touch the core of my being. And to Patty, Ralph, and Linda, three friends who also are family. Your constant support and caring sustain me in wonderful ways.

Laurie

THE PORTFOLIO ORGANIZER

SUCCEEDING WITH PORTFOLIOS IN YOUR CLASSROOM

FOREWORD

In the age of accountability and the improvement of student learning, a new and powerful set of skills has come on the scene. We call it "assessment literacy" (Hargreaves & Fullan, 1998). Assessment literacy refers to the capacity of teachers (individually, but especially together) to (1) examine and critically understand achievement and performance data concerning student learning outcomes, (2) develop classroom and school improvement plans based on the data, and directed at improving results, and (3) use their political ability to participate in local debates about the uses and misuses of achievement data in order to be positively influential in using accountability for learning and improvement.

There is a paucity of good literature on the topic of assessment literacy. *The Portfolio Organizer* stands out as a superb contribution to the vital field of accountability for learning. This book is distinguished by the presence and integration of a conceptual framework and a superb array of practical examples. Nearly every key issue is anticipated and addressed in this accessible and clear treatment of a complex topic. The purposes and audience are carefully presented along with corresponding descriptions of samples, sharing of learning, evaluation and grading, and using portfolios for professional development as well as for improving student performance.

The authors have been immersed in pioneering work on portfolios for a decade. They have developed their ideas through work with their own students and through a wide range of research and evaluation projects including new initiatives involving elementary and secondary school students, initial preparation of teachers, and continuous professional development of teachers and administrators. They have learned by grappling with the complex issues of introducing evaluation that simultaneously serves improvement and accountability goals.

The result is a great practical book that can help educators develop their understanding and use of portfolios as a route to reform.

—MICHAEL FULLAN

PREFACE

The Portfolio Organizer evolved from our work in a variety of educational contexts and our belief in the development of high-quality teaching and learning relationships. After 10 years of experimenting and using portfolio in many different ways, we share a passionate belief in the power of portfolios. Our portfolio adventures have included work with teachers, students, parents, and administrators in elementary and secondary schools, with students and professors in universities, as well as with colleagues involved in professional development. Our collective experimentation has illuminated the many productive paths that portfolio assessment can take. Together we have grappled with the nuts and bolts of managing the portfolio process, crafted user-friendly materials, created frameworks for thinking flexibly about the many choices to be made, developed procedures for use across ages and curriculums, and adapted the process to meet the demands of local requirements and standards.

Through our work with diverse groups, we have realized that regardless of the educational setting in which portfolios are used, there are common areas that demand decision making. *The Portfolio Organizer* addresses those areas. We have designed it as a practical tool for critically thinking through the issues in each area and making sound choices that result in optimal learning. It is also a tool that acknowledges the importance of the many relationships that strengthen student learning.

This book provides educators—experienced and inexperienced—with a flexible framework to guide decision making for effective and efficient use of portfolios in classrooms and schools. The decision making provides a coherent conceptual and structural framework for dealing with the broad and complex array of issues educators face when using portfolios in educational settings. As a tool for decision making, this book is designed to assist educators in identifying, organizing, and acting upon the many challenges and possibilities inherent in portfolio implementation. *The Portfolio Organizer* targets major categories of decision making, which are reflected in the first 10 chapters. In the final chapter, we help educators explore how to develop and maintain professional portfolios.

In light of our diversity—and yours—we have not prescribed one way of implementing portfolios. *The Portfolio Organizer* illustrates a range of possibilities. While we have made connections to relevant theory to illustrate powerful dimensions of portfolio assessment, our main focus is on implementation. We want the process to be meaningful and manageable for all participants. Portfolio assessment is not effective if teachers cannot manage it; we offer teachers many practical ideas that can make the process workable for them and their students. For those who say portfolio assessment is challenging, time-consuming, and complex, we agree; but good teaching and learning are all these things. Throughout our experiences with portfolios, our colleagues and students have communicated that both the process and product are meaningful and authentic, and that caring and pride naturally evolve when something genuinely matters.

We hope that in your portfolio journeys you will discover as many treasures, experience as much pleasure, and celebrate as much student success as we have, and we wish you well.

ACKNOWLEDGMENTS

We offer our heartfelt thanks to the following people for their support and encouragement before and during the writing of *The Portfolio Organizer*.

To our families: We are blessed with loving families who are rich threads in the fabric of our lives. Your keen interest and curiosity about our work reflects your care and concern, and we are grateful for all that you do and all that you are.

To Shari Schwartz, Winnie Hunsburger, and Dennis Couperthwaite: Thank you for sharing your portfolio journeys with us with such enthusiasm and delight. We celebrate your hard work, your teaching expertise, and your insatiable appetite for learning.

To valued colleagues who enrich our learning: We thank Michael Fullan, dean of OISE/University of Toronto, for his vision, empowerment, and unending encouragement of others to become change agents. Thanks to the OISE/UT Learning Community preservice team for being valued learning partners. Your capacity to celebrate the successes of students and teammates is remarkable, and your support for one another is constant.

To Craig Hunt and Maureen Ricciuto, along with other friends and colleagues at Dunbarton and Exeter High Schools, thank you for your energy, talent, and willingness to take risks. Your students are fortunate indeed.

To Ann Trakosas: You saw us through technology challenges and provided professional assistance in formatting and correcting drafts of this manuscript. We value your patience, skill, and good nature—you are amazing.

To Joyce McLeod, our editor: Your heartening words of encouragement and tireless dedication to this manuscript meant so much. You always took time from your busy life to respond to our work with promptness, care, and conceptual clarity. Your passion for and commitment to education inspires us. And to John O'Neil, thank you for having confidence in this project.

To the countless teachers and administrators who have contributed to our thinking about portfolios: We appreciate working with you at conferences, workshops, and institutes; we admire your enthusiasm for this profession, your capacity for continuous learning, and your willingness to deal with complex issues.

And finally, but most importantly, to our students: You make teaching the passionate and rewarding profession that it is. You have trusted us, taught us, questioned us, and celebrated with us as we have explored portfolio assessment with you. We thank you for your effort, ownership, and accomplishments. It is a privilege to have been partners with you.

To all, thank you. You are a part of this.

DETERMINING THE BASICS OF STUDENT PORTFOLIOS

KEY IDEAS

- Establishing the goals and overall purpose of the portfolio
- Choosing a type of portfolio
- Considering the audiences for the portfolio
- Determining the time frame for maintaining the portfolio

OVERVIEW

The material in this chapter helps you make decisions about the use and purpose of portfolio assessment in your classroom, school, or district. Focusing on and clarifying your educational goals is crucial groundwork for all other decisions. To define those goals, you'll work through an activity that is designed to identify the purpose of the portfolio. Once the purpose of the portfolio has been determined, a particular type of portfolio—either growth or best work—can be chosen, and the time frame for portfolio maintenance can be set. Through another activity you'll think about the different audiences for students' portfolios and plan to address their various needs. Use the figures to help you make and record key decisions about the purpose, type, audiences, and time frame for your students' portfolios.

ESTABLISHING GOALS AND PURPOSES

Beginning with your broader educational goals will help you focus decision making about the implementation of portfolios in your educational setting and clarify the purpose of the portfolios. Goals often emerge from an external source (state, provincial, or district guidelines) or an internal source (personal philosophy). Goals that are determined by external guidelines usually form the initial basis for classroom instruction and assessment; however, teachers tend to merge these external goals with personal goals that reflect their philosophical and pragmatic orientations. **Activity 1** will help you articulate your "dream goals" for students. See **Figure 1.1** for examples of dream goals, or responses, to **Activity 1**.

Helping students "develop a love of learning," "become self-directed learners," and "have a positive sense of self" are often identified by teachers as the most important goals to achieve with their students. When teachers articulate these or other personal goals, they are better able to select instructional and assessment approaches that will help them and their students achieve both personal goals and external goals. Portfolio assessment enables teachers to meet both personal and external goals because the process of developing a portfolio and the product created can target a variety of goals.

ACTIVITY 1
Identifying Dream Goals

Whether you are implementing portfolio assessment for personal or external reasons, identifying your dream goals will help you and your students maintain focus, direction, and motivation. Use the following steps to think about and share dream goals with other professionals. Samples of responses are shared in **Figure 1.1**.

• Form groups of three teachers. Teacher A serves as the interviewer, B the responder, and C the recorder.

• Teacher A interviews Teacher B, while Teacher C records the response to these questions:
  – What are some things you would like your students to achieve this year?
  – What is your dream goal for your students and why is it important?

• Teachers rotate roles after each interview, until each teacher has been interviewed. (Allow 3-5 minutes for each interview.)

• Discuss how your dream goals will influence instructional and assessment choices.

• Responses can also be shared in a large group.

Identifying the purpose of the portfolio is an essential decision that will influence many facets of organizing the portfolio. Given the importance of this decision, think carefully about the fundamental reasons you are considering the implementation of portfolio assessment. Here are some questions you may want to consider:

• Why am I implementing portfolio assessment? Is it mandated by an external body or is it a personal choice?

• Why do I want to involve students in collecting and evaluating their own work?

• How will portfolios help me achieve my personal goals with my students?

• Is my purpose to show the process and product of work or just the product itself?

• Is my purpose to have students accumulate a sampling of "best work" for admission to a particular program or for employment?

• Is my purpose to carry out large-scale assessment or to report progress and inform instruction at the classroom level?

• Is my purpose to evaluate overall student performance or to target specific areas?

Your answers to these questions will be influenced by the control that you have within your educational setting and will determine the overall purpose of the portfolios. The more that you are able to incorporate your personal goals into the portfolio model, the more ownership and motivation you will feel throughout the process.

Figure 1.1

Sample Responses to Activity 1 (Dream Goals)

The following thoughts are from teachers who identified dream goals for their students. Use their responses
to **Activity 1** to prompt your thinking as you consider your personal goals.

Winnie's Dream Goals

My dream goal for my students is that they begin to take
responsibility for their own learning. I teach middle school students and I often think they come to school expecting to be
told what they have to know and learn. My goal is to help
them find relevance in their learning and recognize the importance of their own ideas, feelings, and questions. I want them
to start making connections between what they are learning in
school and who they are as individuals. To accomplish this goal,
I need to find out for myself what is important to them and
give them opportunities to reflect on what they are learning. I
also need to provide experiences that are meaningful to them,
that excite them, and that tap into their interests and needs.

Portfolios can certainly help me understand my students
better and come to know where their interests are, what their
goals are, and what kinds of experiences they enjoy the most.
Portfolios also give them a way to think about what they are
learning and connect that with their own lives.

Barb's Dream Goals

I would like my high school students to be self-directed learners who are able to identify their own strengths and weaknesses and are able to set realistic goals for themselves. I have
always understood that kids know themselves better than anyone else, yet I haven't always tapped into that knowledge
appropriately. It is usually pretty easy to tell students how they
need to improve, but it is so much more powerful if they can
articulate that themselves. My dream goal this semester is for
my kids to say, "These are things I am good at, these are things
I am not good at, and this is how I am going to improve." Then
they can work toward their goals as I assist them in that
process.

My dream goal will influence my instructional and assessment choices because I need to teach my students how to
self-evaluate more effectively as they acquire the knowledge
and skills necessary for each class. My assessment approaches
will have to include giving students many opportunities to
practice self-evaluation and I will have to share some of the
"power" in the overall assessment and evaluation process. My
students' judgments must count for something if they are
going to become more self-directed in their learning.

TYPES OF PORTFOLIOS

After identifying the reasons for using portfolio
assessment, you need to determine what type of
portfolio best suits your needs. The literature on
the types, or categories, of portfolio assessment
shows many different ways that portfolios have
been conceptualized. For example, Danielson and
Abrutyn (1997) identify three major types of portfolios: working portfolios, display portfolios, and
assessment portfolios. Seely (1996) identifies four
types of portfolios: showcase, documentation,
evaluation, and process. Burke, Fogarty, and
Belgrad (1994) discuss three major categories for
portfolios: personal, academic, and professional.
Campbell, Cignetti, Melenyzer, Nettles, and
Wyman (1997) elaborate on a working and a presentation portfolio in their discussion of portfolios.

Although the conceptualizations of these
authors are different, the common theme in determining the type of portfolio to use is that "it is
important for educators to be clear about their
goals, the reasons they are engaging in a portfolio
project, and the intended audience for the

portfolios" (Danielson & Abrutyn, 1997, p. 1). To simplify your decision making, think about portfolio types by focusing on two major classifications: best work portfolio and growth portfolio.

BEST WORK PORTFOLIO

This type of portfolio highlights and shows evidence of the best work of learners. Frequently, this type of portfolio is called a display or showcase portfolio. For students, best work is often associated with pride and a sense of accomplishment and can result in a desire to share their work with others. Best work can include both product and process. It is often correlated with the amount of effort that learners have invested in their work. A major advantage of this type of portfolio is that learners can select items that reflect their highest level of learning and can explain why these items represent their best effort and achievement. Best work portfolios are used for the following purposes:

Student Achievement. Students may select a given number of entries (e.g., 10) that reflect their best effort or achievement (or both) in a course of study. The portfolio can be presented in a student-led parent conference or at a community open house. As students publicly share their excellent work, work they have chosen and reflected upon, the experience may enhance their self-esteem.

Post-Secondary Admissions. The preparation of a post-secondary portfolio targets work samples from high school that can be submitted for consideration in the process of admission to college or university. This portfolio should show evidence of a range of knowledge, skills, and attitudes, and may highlight particular qualities relevant to specific programs. Many colleges and universities are adding portfolios to the initial admissions process while others are using them to determine particular placements once students are admitted.

Employability. The audience for this portfolio is an employer. This collection of work needs to be focused on specific knowledge, skills, and attitudes necessary for a particular job or career. The school-to-work movements in North America are influencing an increase in the use of employability portfolios. The Conference Board of Canada (1992), for example, outlines the academic, personal management, and teamwork skills that are the foundation of a high-quality Canadian workforce. An employability portfolio is an excellent vehicle for showcasing these skills.

GROWTH PORTFOLIO

A growth portfolio demonstrates an individual's development and growth over time. Development can be focused on academic or thinking skills, content knowledge, self-knowledge, or any area that is important in your setting. A focus on growth connects directly to identified educational goals and purposes. When growth is emphasized, a portfolio will contain evidence of struggle, failure, success, and change. The growth will likely be an uneven journey of highs and lows, peaks and valleys, rather than a smooth continuum. What is significant is that learners recognize growth whenever it occurs and can discern the reasons behind that growth. The goal of a growth portfolio is for learners to see their own changes over time and, in turn, share their journey with others.

A growth portfolio can be culled to extract a best work sample. It also helps learners see how achievement is often a result of their capacity to self-evaluate, set goals, and work over time. Growth portfolios can be used for the following purposes:

Knowledge. This portfolio shows students' growth in knowledge in a particular content area or across several content areas over time. This kind of portfolio can contain samples of both satisfactory and unsatisfactory work, along with reflections to guide further learning.

Skills and Attitudes. This portfolio shows students' growth in skills and attitudes in areas such as academic disciplines, social skills, thinking skills, and work habits. In this type of portfolio, challenges, difficult experiences, and other growth events can be included to demonstrate students' developing skills. In a thinking skills portfolio, for example, students might include evidence showing growth in their ability to recall, comprehend, apply, analyze, synthesize, and evaluate information.

Teamwork. This portfolio demonstrates growth in social skills in a variety of cooperative experiences. Peer responses and evaluations are vital elements in this portfolio model, along with self-evaluations. Evidence of changing attitudes resulting from team experiences can also be included, especially as expressed in self-reflections and peer evaluations.

Career. This portfolio helps students identify personal strengths related to potential career choices. The collection can be developed over several years, perhaps beginning in middle school and continuing throughout high school. The process of selecting pieces over time empowers young people to make appropriate educational choices leading toward meaningful careers. Career portfolios may contain items from outside the school setting that substantiate students' choices and create a holistic view of the students as learners and people. This type of portfolio may be modified for employment purposes.

CONSIDERING THE AUDIENCES

At one time teachers were the sole participants in assessment decisions, and students and parents were viewed as the recipients of those decisions (Shaklee, Barbour, Ambrose, & Hansford, 1997). Today, however, educators are more actively engaging a wide array of audiences in the assessment process. These audiences are not only rich sources of ongoing information, but also bring diverse perspectives to students' learning. Portfolio assessment is a valuable tool for building bridges and creating partnerships with many audiences, or stakeholders, resulting in better learning opportunities for all students. As Shaklee and colleagues note, "The cast of stakeholders may vary from program to program or from teacher to teacher and from time to time. The important factor is that teachers and students define a series of multiple stakeholders in order to provide a broad panorama of the students' abilities" (1997, p. 44).

Many different audiences, or stakeholders, may have a role in the portfolio assessment process. Audiences vary, depending on your particular setting, goals, and purposes. Primary audiences usually include students, parents, teachers, and administrators. Knowing the assessment, evaluation, and grading needs and concerns of these groups will help you implement a portfolio process that is aligned with the needs of your audiences. **Activity 2** will help you assess each group's needs; **Figure 1.2** captures the needs and concerns generated by a parent while participating in **Activity 2**.

Potential audiences may vary according to the purpose and type of portfolio used. For example, the student creating a best-work employability portfolio needs to consider employers as a primary audience. On the other hand, a growth portfolio focused on academic skills might involve peers in the classroom, other teachers (e.g., a resource teacher), and parents. Ways that teachers can engage a variety of partners in the portfolio process, including creative ways for students to share their learning, will be explored in Chapter 7.

ACTIVITY 2
Identifying Needs and Concerns of Audiences

What audiences will your students' portfolios reach? What are their needs
and concerns? How can you and your students meet those needs? Use this
activity to anticipate the needs and concerns of the various audiences that
may participate in the portfolio process.

• Form groups of four participants, including teachers and administrators when possible.

• For each group, divide a piece of paper into quarters to use as a recording sheet. Use one label for each section: students, parents, teachers, and administrators.

• Ask each participant to record the group's ideas for one section.

• Allow about 3 minutes to brainstorm and record ideas in each of the four sections. The ideas should be focused on the needs and concerns of each audience (students, parents, teachers, and administrators), regarding assessment, evaluation, and grading. For example, the recorder can ask the group the following questions:

–What are the needs and concerns of [students] regarding assessment (gathering data)?
–What are the needs and concerns of [students] regarding evaluation (judging merits)?
–What are the needs and concerns of [students] regarding grading (assigning values to symbols for reporting)?

• At the end of the group process, facilitate a whole-group discussion to identify key ideas related to each audience. The following questions may guide discussion:
–What are the common concerns and needs across all audiences?
–How do the concerns and needs differ across the audiences?
–What potential contributions could each audience make to the portfolio process?

TIME FRAME

The time frame of portfolio maintenance is a key factor influenced by decisions about goals, purposes, and type of portfolio. For example, if a growth portfolio is being used to document learning across the entire curriculum, then a full-year time frame may be most appropriate. For a high school teacher using a best work portfolio focused on algebra and problem-solving skills, however, a term or semester portfolio may be adequate. For teachers just beginning to experiment with portfolios, a shorter time frame may be advisable (e.g., a best work portfolio in social studies for six weeks). A short-term experience can build early success for the teacher and can help build confidence for future refinement and expansion.

As you select a time frame, consider students' familiarity with portfolio assessment. Students who have had experience creating portfolios will allow the teacher to proceed quickly through the initial stage of portfolio introduction because they understand many of the concepts related to portfolio use. Students with some portfolio experience will also be able to handle long-term portfolios because they are more comfortable with self-directed learning.

Use **Planner A** on pp. 8–9 to record your decisions as you work through this chapter. Keeping a log or journal of the decision-making process can help you implement portfolio assessment in your classroom and assist you in evaluating and modifying your portfolio assessment plans.

FIGURE 1.2

Sample Response to Activity 2 (Needs and Concerns)

When you think about portfolios, you must also consider the audiences your students' portfolios will reach. The following comments from a parent illustrate a few of the needs and concerns that may emerge from the discussion outlined in **Activity 2**.

A Parent's Needs and Concerns

As my children progressed through elementary school and high school, I always worried that the assessments they faced did not demonstrate their unique strengths, talents, or weaknesses. Of course, every mother believes that her son or daughter is wonderful and hopes that the teacher will see what she sees. It can be easy to feel that a test or a prescriptive assignment doesn't allow your child to really demonstrate what he can do. I worry that busy teachers will not have the time to really get to know my child. Some children are very forthcoming about what they like, what they are good at, or what scares them. But others are much more reticent. I want teachers to get to know who my children are as individuals.

PLANNER A
SUMMARIZING PORTFOLIO DECISIONS

Use this figure to record the decisions you have made about your students' portfolios. This summary of your planning will guide your next steps.

Educational Goals

List documents that contain mandated educational goals. Specifically check school, district, and state or provincial documents.

_____

_____

_____

_____

_____

List personal dream goals that you generated in **Activity 1**. Add additional goals, as appropriate.

_____

_____

_____

_____

_____

Purpose

Based on your educational goals, what are the key purposes of the portfolio?

_____

_____

_____

_____

_____

_____

Type

What type of portfolio have you chosen?

☐ Best work portfolio   ☐ Growth portfolio

What is the focus of the portfolio (e.g., a particular subject area, a unit of content, work habits)?

_____

_____

_____

Record your reasons for choosing the type and focus of the portfolio.

_____

_____

_____

_____

_____

Audiences

List key audiences that may be part of your portfolio assessment process. Summarize the concerns and issues for each audience and any ideas you have to address these concerns and issues.

_____

_____

_____

_____

_____

_____

Time Frame

Decide the time frame for maintaining the portfolios. For example, do you intend the portfolio to be focused on a unit that will stretch over a few weeks or the entire school year? Record your decision.

☐ Unit (___ weeks)   ☐ Semester or term   ☐ Full year   ☐ Multiyear

☐ Other (specify: _____)

SELECTING CATEGORIES FOR ENTRIES

OVERVIEW

This chapter helps you define appropriate categories for your portfolio model and provides many practical examples for use in a variety of settings. The categories you choose are key to organizing the portfolio process because they help learners make selections for their portfolios. Use the figures to guide you in making and recording decisions and ideas about the categories for your students' portfolios.

DETERMINING CATEGORIES

Whether you choose a best work or growth portfolio as the most appropriate type for your students, your next step is to identify the categories around which the portfolio will be organized (e.g., subject areas, problem solving, types of writing). Choosing specific categories ensures a focused

selection of entries. For example, in a best-work writing portfolio, students may need to show achievement in short story fiction, short story non-fiction, persuasive essay, and poetry.

Activity 3 will help you think through issues related to the selection of portfolio categories. **Figure 2.1** shows how one teacher has thought through choosing her portfolio categories.

EXAMPLES OF PORTFOLIO CATEGORIES

Considering your strengths and priorities will help you determine the categories for portfolio organization. By clearly defining categories, you increase the chances that students' portfolios will be organized easily and effectively. Such clarity also ensures that you have a solid conceptual framework to guide students in collecting learning samples.

There are two ways to think about forming categories. One way is to consider broad categories that reflect the framework you use for curriculum planning and implementation. For example, if your framework for planning includes a major subject area such as language arts, the broad categories for entries might include reading, writing, and speaking. Determining broad categories may be as simple as listing what you spend the most time on throughout the instructional year. Alternatively, you can consider using more specific categories

ACTIVITY 3
Identifying Strengths and Priorities

Use these steps to help you think about using personal strengths and priorities of your instructional program to determine effective categories for organizing portfolios. First, find a partner who teaches the same grade level or common subject area. Ask your partner to record your responses to the following questions and then reverse roles. See **Figure 2.1** for sample responses to this activity.

1. What are the areas or special aspects of your program that you most enjoy teaching?

2. Is there a specific curriculum area or focus that your school or district has identified as a priority for your class or classes?

3. Is there an area of your program in which you would like to develop opportunities for student reflection, self-evaluation, or self-directed learning?

4. What is your time frame for collecting portfolio entries? How does the time frame affect your choice of categories?

5. What preferences or ideas for grouping or organizing your students' portfolio entries do you have?

Read the interview notes your partner recorded. Summarize your strengths and priorities.

such as narrative writing, poetry, and expository writing—categories that may be related to concentrated periods of study.

Figure 2.2 and **Figure 2.3** give practical examples of entry categories that have been used successfully and can be readily adapted to different grade levels and subject areas. The samples target broad categories **(Figure 2.2)** and specific categories **(Figure 2.3)** for portfolio entries, and offer brief explanations of the ideas. These lists will help you consider the many possibilities for portfolio organization.

Portfolios can be organized using other teaching and learning ideas, such as learning styles or multiple intelligences. The categories shown in

Figure 2.4 (p. 15) are based on Howard Gardner's theory of multiple intelligences (Gardner, 1983). In his early work, Gardner makes the argument that intelligence is pluralized, in that there is more than one type of intelligence. In his ongoing conceptualization, Gardner treats intelligence as a set of human potentials. He emphasizes this notion by offering a reasonable list of what the several intelligences might be. Gardner continues to argue that these intelligences work in combination, that all of us possess these intelligences, and that all of us can use them productively (Gardner, in Lazear, 1991). His theory resonates with many teachers because it connects so clearly with their own teaching and learning experiences (Scherer, 1999).

FIGURE 2.1

Sample Response to Activity 3 (Strengths and Priorities)

While thinking about her strengths and priorities in **Activity 3**, Barb wrote the following assessment of her math course.

Barb's Thoughts

In my math course for 10th graders, I have to cover a great deal of prescribed content, focusing primarily on algebraic concepts. What I try to do is to incorporate multiple intelligences (MI) into my program. I want students to increase their awareness of their own particular strengths and to apply those strengths to learning math in different ways. My school district has provided some professional development in MI, but it's up to individual teachers to apply the theory with their students.

I think that an emphasis on MI will encourage my students to practice intrapersonal and interpersonal skills as they reflect on their work and share it with their peers. If they can demonstrate their learning in creative ways (e.g., design a visual mind map for review purposes), I think they will enjoy the learning process and feel that they have more control over how they master key material.

I am going to have students begin collecting entries two weeks into the semester and finalize their portfolios about three weeks before final exams. The timing allows them to settle into the course before we begin the portfolio process and to complete their portfolios before other end-of-term projects are due. I will also have time to evaluate the portfolios

before the end of the year. The number of entries depends on how much class time we have for self-evaluation training, peer responses, and the motivation of individual students in completing timely reflections.

I am going to give my students two choices for how they will categorize their portfolio entries. They may choose broad categories such as multiple intelligences and provide evidence of how they used each of the eight intelligences throughout the course. On the other hand, they may target categories based on individual units in the course, such as real numbers and polynomials. I suspect that most students will select the latter system because it is an easy, straightforward way to organize their entries. They like to track their own progress from the beginning of the course to the end.

I have learned to give my students choices as often as possible. When I began using portfolios, I tended to control a great deal of what went into them and how and when students responded to their work. Through the years, however, I've realized that students value the process and the final product more when they can participate in decision making. How they categorize their portfolio entries, therefore, is not as important as making decisions that are meaningful to them.

Consequently, as teachers have explored the connections between Gardner's theory and their own practices, many have discovered that any topic and concept can be taught or learned using several intelligences. For teachers using multiple intelligences in their classrooms, Gardner's framework works well as a basis for portfolio organization.

Because entry categories create the organizational backbone of the portfolio, they should be identified in some way, either in a table of contents (see Chapter 6) or on the reflection sheet that accompanies each learning sample in the portfolio (see Chapter 5). Such identification assists readers of the portfolio in understanding the framework guiding the portfolio contents and prepares students to explain their reasons for their entry selections to parents, peers, principals, and other interested audiences. Use **Planner B** (p. 16) to record your ideas for categorizing entries in your portfolio model.

FIGURE 2.2

Broad Categories for Portfolio Entries

If your students choose to organize their portfolios by broad categories, here's how they can link broad categories to specific entries.

SUBJECT	BROAD CATEGORIES FOR PORTFOLIO ENTRIES	EXAMPLES OF ENTRIES
Math	–Abstract Thinking –Computation –Problem Solving ⟶	(8th grade) –problem sets with detailed solutions –a videotaped presentation showing the solution to a real-life problem –a detailed analysis of a problem using a visual organization tool, such as a Venn diagram –writing selection in which students describe their approach to solving a particular problem
Reading and Language Arts	–Writing –Speaking –Listening –Viewing –Comprehension ⟶	(2nd grade) –audiotape samples of students reading stories –mind map depicting the sequence of events in a favorite story –mind map of settings and characters in a favorite story –videotape of student enacting a scene from a favorite story –list of personal vocabulary words illustrated and defined by student
Employability Skills	–Academic Skills –Personal Management Skills –Teamwork Skills ⟶	(High school) –peer evaluation of participation in a cooperative activity –a log of group decisions and actions for a group investigation –an individual report outlining personal contributions to a team presentation

Some ideas adapted from Conference Board of Canada, Corporate Council on Education (1992)

FIGURE 2.3

Using Specific Categories for Portfolio Organization

Start with these ideas of specific categories to help you envision the possibilities for your students.
These categories were used with 10th grade students.

SUBJECT	SPECIFIC CATEGORIES FOR PORTFOLIO ENTRIES	EXAMPLES OF ENTRIES
Math	Number sense	
	Geometry and spatial sense	–corrected algebra test –a list of English expressions translated into algebraic terms –sample of an Escher drawing
	Measurement	
	Patterns and Algebra	
	Data management and probability	
Writing	Grammar	
	Punctuation	
	Spelling	
	Word use and vocabulary building	
	Visual presentation	–best writing sample –variety of writing formats appropriate for different purposes (e.g., letter, e-mail message, chart) –writing sample that incorporates a title and subheadings to enhance organization
Personal Management Skills	Adaptability	
	Positive attitude and behavior	
	Responsibility	–evaluation by an employer from a work program –a community service certificate –attendance record –a self-evaluation of contributions to a group project

FIGURE 2.4

Using Multiple Intelligences to Organize Portfolios

How are students going to organize their portfolios? This sample shows how you can use multiple intelligences as categories. Students may use the intelligences as broad categories or as specific categories. Here's an example to guide you and your students.

BROAD CATEGORY: MULTIPLE INTELLIGENCES	EXAMPLES OF ENTRIES

Spatial	Middle school level
	    —diorama of vegetation regions
	    —map of local community
	    —architectural plan for energy-efficient building

Linguistic	
Musical	

Bodily-Kinesthetic	Middle school level
	    —videotape of class skit for social studies
	    —photo of self-constructed model of a complex geometric shape
	    —evaluation of an original dance routine

Interpersonal	

Intrapersonal	Middle school level
	    —buddy reading log
	    —peer evaluation of group performance
	    —research plan for a group investigation

Logical-Mathematical	
Naturalist	

SPECIFIC CATEGORY: SPATIAL INTELLIGENCE	EXAMPLES OF ENTRIES
Patterns	

Images and pictures	Middle school level
	    -drawings of images seen under a microscope
	    -mind maps depicting chapters in a novel
	    -a poster or collage illustrating historical events

Colors	
Designs	

PLANNER B
CATEGORIES FOR ENTRIES

Use this figure to capture your thinking regarding the entry categories you plan to use in the portfolio model. Targeting specific categories or using categories in which you are more skilled and comfortable facilitates a smooth start and a manageable process if you are just beginning to use portfolio assessment. A word of advice—the fewer categories, the easier the portfolio process will be for both you and your students.

Record the categories you plan to use for portfolio entries.

Identify the reasons you have chosen each category.

1. _____

1. _____
   _____
   _____

2. _____

2. _____
   _____
   _____

3. _____

3. _____
   _____
   _____

4. _____

4. _____
   _____
   _____

5. _____

5. _____
   _____
   _____

IDENTIFYING LEARNING EXPECTATIONS AND CRITERIA

KEY IDEAS

- Understanding criteria
- Selecting criteria for successful portfolios

OVERVIEW

This chapter helps you identify the areas to consider in determining criteria that are appropriate for selecting entries and evaluating the overall portfolio. Use the information and sample criteria to think critically about appropriate criteria for your model. Record and refine your decisions about criteria relevant to your portfolio model on **Planner C**.

WHY CRITERIA ARE CRITICAL

To begin with the end in mind means to start with a clear understanding of your destination. It means to know where you're going so that you better understand where you are now so that the steps you take are always in the right direction.

—*Stephen Covey*
Seven Habits of Highly Effective
People: Powerful Lessons in
Personal Change, *1989, p. 98*

When you and your students are clear about the criteria for selecting entries at the beginning of the portfolio process, the process tends to result in a fair, focused, and efficient assessment. Basically, criteria are indicators of success. Although decisions regarding criteria may evolve, begin by asking yourself how you will use criteria in assessing the portfolio. Will you assess each entry for how well it meets established criteria? Or will you assess the portfolio on how well the collection as a whole meets the established criteria? Evaluating how individual learning samples meet criteria is a part of a teacher's overall assessment and evaluation responsibilities, therefore assessing individual entries in a portfolio is a familiar practice for most teachers. Evaluating how a portfolio as a whole collection meets the established criteria, however, if unfamiliar and challenging for many teachers. Assessing the entire portfolio against criteria demands the review of many learning samples and reflections to determine if the criteria have been met. In Chapter 9, examples show how criteria can be developed into a rubric identifying varying levels of performance or standards for evaluative and grading purposes. Because it is important to consider the portfolio as an entire collection of work that reflects many aspects of the learner, we will help you identify criteria for evaluating the portfolio as a whole.

Your choice of learning standards and objectives, which also drive the goals, outcomes, and expectations for a course of study, is key to establishing criteria for evaluating individual portfolio entries and the entire portfolio.

IDENTIFYING POSSIBLE CRITERIA

To begin, review the learning expectations for the course of study or focus area you have selected for portfolio assessment. Review any significant guidelines or curriculum documents provided by your state, province, or school district. Based on your review of documents relevant to a 7th grade Language Arts portfolio, for example, you might identify a category of Oral and Visual Communication. Information specified in the documents will likely provide direction for the criteria to target in your students' portfolios. For example, teachers in Ontario expect that 7th grade students will create a variety of media works (e.g., a class newspaper, a story board, or a radio documentary) and will ask questions and discuss different aspects of ideas to clarify their thinking (e.g., use analogies and comparisons to develop and clarify ideas). Accordingly, you might determine the criteria to be (1) variety of entries, and (2) evidence of higher-level thinking.

After setting tentative criteria, review your thoughts from Chapter 2, especially **Planner B**, and your decisions about categories for portfolio entries. Ensure that the categories (and type of portfolio) align with the potential criteria you are considering. For example, in the Mathematics Portfolio **(Figure 2.2)**, broad categories were identified: Abstract Thinking, Computation, and Problem Solving. Criteria relevant to those broad categories might be (1) evidence of understanding, (2) perseverance, and (3) communication of ideas. For the Employability Portfolio, three broad categories were listed: Academic Skills, Personal Management Skills, and Teamwork Skills. Appropriate criteria for these categories might include (1) self-assessment, (2) goal setting, (3)

performance, and (4) completeness.

While identifying criteria, also consider your personal beliefs about what could best demonstrate students' learning, the time available, and students' interests and needs. Combining these perspectives helps you select meaningful and important criteria.

The following sample criteria can be easily adapted to a variety of settings. As you review this list, consider which criteria best suit your requirements and your students' needs.

- completeness
- creativity and originality
- evidence of understanding
- depth of reflection
- knowledge of content
- knowledge of concepts
- accuracy of information
- perseverance
- quality of product
- self-assessment and goal setting
- variety of entries
- visual appeal
- cross-curricular connections
- neatness
- organization and presentation
- communication of ideas
- problem solving

(adapted from Burke, Fogarty, & Belgrad, 1994, p.73)

As you contemplate possible criteria, remember that the process must be manageable for you and your students. One key to managing the portfolio process is limiting the number of criteria that you select. For beginning portfolio learners, choose no more than four criteria. Teachers and students with portfolio experience may wish to target a few more criteria. Also consider the issues related to learners sharing portfolios with other audiences; four to seven criteria should be sufficient to communicate many facets of the learner to the audiences. Too many criteria may result in a somewhat cumbersome model that overwhelms the learner and loses focus. Also, if audiences other than peers and the teacher are involved in the process, a limited number of criteria increases the likelihood that the less experienced audiences will understand the ideas involved. Chapter 7 explores sharing the learning with a variety of audiences. Use **Activity 4** as an initial step in consolidating your thinking about appropriate criteria for the portfolio model you have chosen. Working with the list of criteria supplied in this chapter may help you to get started or you may choose to read **Figure 3.1**, a sample response to **Activity 4**.

Planner C (p. 23) guides you in selecting the criteria appropriate for your portfolio model.

SELECTING CRITERIA

Teachers new to the portfolio process may find comfort in choosing criteria themselves and ensuring student understanding of the criteria. When students and teachers have had experience with portfolios, however, they can collaborate in prioritizing and selecting portfolio criteria. For example, the teacher may choose two criteria, while students choose two additional criteria. Negotiating

---

ACTIVITY 4
Identifying Wows and Woes of Portfolio Criteria

Use this activity to help you weigh the advantages and disadvantages of the criteria you are considering for your portfolio model.
Find a partner and review the list of criteria outlined in this chapter or use your own ideas. Each of you should select three criteria and work together to generate lists of the advantages ("wows") and disadvantages ("woes") of using each criterion. Remember to consider factors such as time, experience, age of learners, and your familiarity with criteria.

	Criteria	Wows	Woes
1.			
2.			
3.			
4.			
5.			
6.			

FIGURE 3.1

Sample Responses to Activity 4 (Wows and Woes)

Use these sample responses to consider different aspects of the criteria chosen by these teachers and to help you critique your own criteria. Refer to **Activity 4** for an explanation.

Winnie's Wows and Woes of Chosen Criteria (Middle school)

Criteria	Wows	Woes
Quality of reflections	• encourages students to approach reflection seriously • helps students understand that they can learn from work after it is complete • emphasizes the portfolio as not just a collection of good work, but as a picture of students as learners	• some students may have difficulty articulating what they have learned from a specific piece of work
Peer responses	• encourages students to share their work with a wider range of peers • encourages students to respond to others sensitively and constructively • provides students with an opportunity to see how others are reflecting on their work and to see what others are including in their portfolios	• students may not always feel safe sharing their work with peers, or may feel shy about sharing their work • students may not feel comfortable about responding to work they feel has been done poorly or that they do not understand
Neatness and organization	• encourages students to take care of their work • eases teacher's evaluation of portfolio • eases a student's presentation of portfolio to others	• some students may be able to reflect deeply on their work, but not organize it well • neatness and tidiness does not always reflect quality

---

the selection of criteria increases students' investment and helps them view assessment as a collaborative endeavor. Students' participation in setting criteria builds ownership, accountability, and involvement in the entire learning process. In addition, when students participate in choosing criteria, they view the process as fair and meaningful because they understand what is expected of them and they can target what will be evaluated.

The following example highlights a high school mathematics portfolio targeting best work. The specific categories the teacher focused on were based on course units, including Number Sense and Numeration, Geometry and Spatial Sense, Measurement, Patterns and Algebra, and Data Management and Probability. The teacher selected the following criteria:
- evidence of understanding
- communication of ideas and solutions
- completeness

FIGURE 3.1 (continued)

Barb's Wows and Woes of Chosen Criteria (High school)

Criteria	Wows	Woes
Presentation and visual appeal	• enables students who are weaker in mathematical computation but stronger visually or artistically to demonstrate their skills • encourages students to write neat solutions to problems • allows for conversation about the importance of "first impressions" • enhances organizational skills	• portfolio may look great, but have weak content • neatness of writing should not matter too much if the content is correct
Variety of entries	• ensures that portfolio contains more than one type of learning sample (e.g., not just unit tests) • encourages students to value all aspects of their learning (e.g., a good homework exercise is as important as a quiz) • provides a more comprehensive portrait of a student	• students may choose entries that they don't really value just to satisfy this criterion • repetition in types of entries may still give a fair portrait of the student • may not provide enough focus or direction for some students
Self-assessment and goal setting	• highlights growth over time • encourages a focus on goals and analyses of whether those goals are reached • shifts emphasis away from grades to what students have learned	• students set goals that are too easy or too difficult to reach, diminishing the value of the experience • may increase chances of phony reflections (sometimes students will say what they think you want to hear) • there may not be enough time during the semester to allow students to practice self-reflection and self-assessment

• organization
• variety of entries

Note that the criteria chosen are from the sample list of criteria (see bulleted list, p. 18). For this particular portfolio model, the teacher based the choice of criteria on curriculum requirements, personal beliefs about what best demonstrates students' learning, and feedback from students about what they valued in their own learning. For example, the teacher chose "evidence of understanding" because the curriculum for this math course necessitated that students demonstrate comprehension of major concepts in the course (e.g., adding and subtracting integers, and working with polynomials). The teacher also chose the "com-

munication of ideas and solutions" because she believes that clearly articulated solutions to mathematical problems are necessary and important. Students chose "organization" because they felt confident that they could demonstrate this skill effectively and were allowed choice in organizing their portfolios. The other criteria were choices negotiated between the teacher and students.

Obviously, the criteria vary greatly from one class to another, from one school to another, and from one district to another. In part, the criteria depend on the degree of control that you and your students have over the process and on the amount of collaboration among the stakeholders. Getting feedback from students and professional colleagues at the end of each term or year in which portfolio assessment is used can help you refine your choices. You'll need to experiment with criteria to discover which are appropriate and which need to be modified for future portfolio models.

Teachers and students new to the portfolio process are sometimes confused about whether criteria are used for entry selection or evaluation purposes. The answer is that criteria for a portfolio that will be judged in its entirety can serve both purposes. The criteria influence students' selections of appropriate entries and provide a basis for the evaluation of the entire collection of work. For example, if "variety of entries" is a criterion, students will ensure that they have a variety of learning samples in their portfolios. "Variety of entries" will also be one criterion by which the teacher and students evaluate the portfolios. Determining levels of performance based on the selected criteria will be discussed in Chapter 9, along with an outline of a process for developing a rubric.

Whether or not a portfolio is graded, what matters is that learners begin the process with a clear sense of the criteria for selecting and reflecting on their work.

PLANNER C
SELECTING CRITERIA

Follow the process outlined below to select appropriate criteria for your portfolio model.
Share your final choices with a colleague and articulate the rationale for your choices.
Verbalizing your rationale helps you develop clarity and focus and allows you to practice the skill
of justifying your professional decisions.

List key learning standards and objectives that you want to target for your students.

1. _____

_____

2. _____

_____

3. _____

_____

List the broad or specific categories for portfolio entries you've identified (see **Planner B,** p. 16).

1. _____

_____

2. _____

_____

3. _____

_____

4. _____

_____

Identify possible criteria for evaluating portfolios that are appropriate for the above learning standards
and objectives.

1. _____   5. _____

2. _____   6. _____

3. _____   7. _____

4. _____   8. _____

Narrow your list of criteria to a workable number.

1. _____   4. _____

2. _____   5. _____

3. _____

LEARNING 4 SAMPLES

KEY IDEAS

- Defining learning samples
- Identifying appropriate types of learning samples
- Selecting learning samples for growth and best work portfolios

OVERVIEW

This chapter helps you define learning samples and engages you in generating examples for your portfolio model. As you work through the activities, consider the types of learning opportunities in your classroom and new possibilities created by the portfolio process itself. A list of potential learning samples is provided to spark your thinking and several questions are posed to guide you in selecting samples.

DEFINING LEARNING SAMPLES

Learning samples are student-produced products (e.g., a theme paper) and evidence of learning processes may include revised drafts and outlines of the theme paper. An important distinction between a portfolio learning sample and a portfolio entry is that a complete entry includes an element of student reflection (see Chapter 5). Thus, a portfolio entry is a learning sample *plus* a reflection on that sample. The reflective process transforms a collection of learning samples into a rich source of data because student reflection provide a more comprehensive and meaningful picture of individual learning. The collection of entries constitutes a portfolio.

IDENTIFYING APPROPRIATE LEARNING SAMPLES

Learning samples may be selected for a variety of reasons. For example, a student may choose a sample because it connects to a particular category and fits a specific criterion. A learning sample may be chosen from work already complete or may be a new product specifically designed for the portfolio. The range of learning samples that can be included in a portfolio is endless, given the diverse goals, purposes, categories, and criteria on which portfolios can focus. The type of portfolio chosen influences the kind of learning samples that will go into the portfolio. A best work portfolio will contain polished pieces that reflect the student's best efforts. A growth portfolio, on the other hand, will include comparative learning samples that reflect the process of learning and growth over time. Portraying growth often takes the form of presenting snapshots of the stages a learner goes through to produce a final product (such as revised versions of a theme paper, oral report, or dramatic performance).

As you think about the types of learning samples students might include in a portfolio, start by considering the types of classwork, homework, and projects that you assign. Implementing portfolios in your classroom adds a new dimension to your assessment practices, but the process will be more manageable if you incorporate into the portfolio meaningful learning samples that already exist as part of your program. For students, meaningful learning samples will include those that allow them to express their personal interests and values. Below are some suggestions of learning samples focused on the two major types of portfolios, best work and growth. Use the activities and other information in this chapter to consolidate your thinking about possible learning samples.

SELECTING LEARNING SAMPLES

The selection of learning samples should be intricately aligned with the purpose and type of portfolio, the categories and criteria chosen, and the learners' interests and values. With the purpose, type, categories, and criteria established in advance, it becomes easier for a learner to both collect and select learning samples. The type of portfolio and the selection of categories may dictate the kinds of learning samples that are appropriate. Learners working on portfolios with multiple intelligences categories, for example, would incorporate samples related to the intelligences. Criteria are relevant, too. If a multiple intelligences portfolio includes the criterion of "completeness," the learner needs to ensure that there are learning samples representing all of the intelligences.

WHO DECIDES?

The learner needs to take primary responsibility for the selection process, although teachers and others will be involved. Depending on the type of portfolio and its purpose, the control over learning sample selection may vary. For example, if the portfolios are mandated by the state or province, the required types of learning samples may be dictated and the learner may have limited control over what goes into the portfolio. On the other hand, for a class-based literacy portfolio, a student can have more choice in which learning samples are selected to meet the identified learning expectations. In a cooperative context of shared control, a teacher and student may negotiate which learning samples best meet the criteria or standards established.

Peers, parents, and family members can be instrumental in the selection process. By having these additional people make suggestions and provide feedback on individual learning products or processes, the learner is better prepared to make choices. In addition, students learn to value the opinions of others while getting comparative views to help them become better at self-evaluation.

LOGISTICS OF SELECTION

Learners can carry out the selection process in many different ways and at several different intervals or times. Choosing methods that help students make good choices is a key consideration for the teacher. The following ideas may help you to think creatively about the selection processes to use with your students:

- Brainstorm ideas for learning samples as a class; students can think about what they want in their portfolios based on a unit or program of study. Using the results of the class exercise, students can select samples for their own portfolios.

- Use independent class time as an opportunity for students to select potential learning samples. Create a routine for selection by scheduling independent time, perhaps once every two weeks. During this time, students are expected to choose a learning sample for reflection and possible inclusion in their portfolios.

- Schedule portfolio round-robins (oral sharing of portfolios) or partner interviews (pairs of students asking questions of each other). To prepare for these exercises, students select specific learning samples and produce accompanying reflections. Similarly, some class time might be devoted to partners sharing particular entries.

- Host a portfolio day during which students gather in small groups to share recent learning samples and reflections.

- Halfway through the time frame set for collecting samples, have students select appropriate entries and use these to help establish goals for future work. The time frame may coincide with midsemester reporting in high schools or report card distribution in elementary schools.

- At the end of the unit or term, direct students to review their learning samples and select a range to include in their portfolios. You may structure the process, for example, by limiting students to five samples that reflect growth over time.

- Meet with each student (or with small groups of students) at the end of each unit and collaborate on identifying a range of learning samples that are appropriate for the portfolio.

- At the end of a year, cull entries to create cumulative portfolios that stay with students throughout their school years.

BEST WORK PORTFOLIO: POSSIBLE LEARNING SAMPLES

If you and your students have chosen a best work portfolio, the types of learning samples included should be edited, polished pieces reflecting best effort and superior skills. For a best work portfolio with multiple intelligences categories, for example, students might include items related to each of the intelligences, such as a detailed mind map that summarizes unit learning, a song they've written and performed, a math test with the highest grade or highest-quality work, and a video of an excellent performance in physical education. For a best work portfolio that is subject-based, students might include the following types of polished learning samples focused on key subject areas:

LANGUAGE ARTS

- polished, written response to literature
- original poem, narrative, short story, or myth
- original script of a skit or scene
- Venn diagram comparing and contrasting characters in a novel
- artistic representation of a dramatic scene
- formal essay
- character study

SOCIAL SCIENCES

- letter to or from a historical character
- analysis of newspaper clippings from a historical event
- review of a historically based film
- biography of a historical character
- diary entries written by student from character's perspective
- time line of key historical events
- letter concerning an issue, accompanied by a response from the party addressed

MATHEMATICS

- solution to an open-ended problem
- three-dimensional model of a geometric shape
- computer-generated graph
- mind map or unit review sheet
- best performance on quiz

CROSS-CURRICULAR

- photograph of a poster designed for class
- response to a newspaper or magazine article
- audiotape or transcript of a speech
- videotape of a performance or presentation
- autobiographical sketch
- computer disk containing relevant information and work

GROWTH PORTFOLIO: POSSIBLE LEARNING SAMPLES

If a growth portfolio is the focus for your students, the learning samples should reflect the students' learning and improvement over time. For a multiple intelligences growth portfolio, students might include items related to each of the intelligences that reflect changes or growth that occurred during a semester or year. Audiotapes of musical performances or of stories read aloud at the start of a semester and at the end of it, for example, would clearly reveal students' growth over that period of time. A photograph of a spatial-visual item, such as a model, might be accompanied by plans and descriptions of the process involved in creating the model.

A subject-based growth portfolio would also contain a variety of learning samples demonstrating growth; items such as the ones listed below are targeted to specific curricular areas:

LANGUAGE ARTS
- personal goal setting for writing, with analysis of strengths and weaknesses
- formal essay or story components, including plan, rough drafts with editing, final draft
- copies of editing and peer responses for other students' writing
- list of books read during the year, along with accompanying comments

SOCIAL SCIENCES
- statistical analysis that makes sense out of data collected throughout the year
- variety of comparisons of primary sources, identifying bias and frame of reference
- collection of newspaper and magazine articles with student's comments relating current events to historical events
- cartoon analyses
- map drawings, done at the beginning of the course and at the end

MATHEMATICS
- variety of graphs with interpretations
- concrete materials or drawings that show understanding and application of a key concept
- examples of best and worst performances on tests, with student's comments articulating the differences between the performances
- examples of growth in using a variety of problem-solving strategies
- variety of work completed in cooperative groups, with explanations of student's role and effort
- detailed problem-solving solutions, with all attempts and rough work included
- samples collected over time that show identification and extension of patterns
- arithmetic drills completed at various times during the year

CROSS-CURRICULAR
- goal-setting sheet, with accompanying plan of action and final analysis of strengths and weaknesses
- examples of best and worst performances on quiz, test, and homework assignments with brief explanations of strengths and weaknesses
- regular self-evaluations of work habits, progress in the course, and skills
- audiotapes and videotapes of performances early and late in the year
- writing samples across the curriculum, done throughout the year

Examining a list of possible learning samples, such as those above, is one way to begin thinking about samples that your students may generate. **Activity 5** presents another way to develop your thinking by taking you through a process of brainstorming and refining your ideas. **Figure 4.1** shows how two teachers consolidated their thinking about learning samples as they engaged in **Activity 5**. Record your decisions on **Planner D**.

ACTIVITY 5
Generating a List of Potential Learning Samples

Use the following activity to create a list of learning samples
students might include in their portfolios.

BRAINSTORMING POTENTIAL LEARNING SAMPLES

List the different types of learning samples your students create or might create including classwork, homework, and projects.

NARROWING THE FOCUS

Examine the list you created above and review the decisions you've made in earlier chapters (e.g., purpose and type of portfolio, categories, and criteria). What learning samples are most appropriate based on the decisions you have made about portfolios? Highlight the appropriate samples on your brainstorming list or copy your best ideas to **Appendix A**.

FIGURE 4.1

Sample Responses to Activity 5 (Potential Learning Samples)

The following ideas are from teachers who used **Activity 5** to generate ideas for learning samples.

Winnie's Ideas

The following ideas are for growth portfolios by 7th graders. The portfolios contain learning samples for all subject areas, with a focus on multiple intelligences.

Brainstorming Potential Learning Samples

- homework assignments
- tests
- finished writing samples (stories, essays, scripts)
- drafts of writing samples
- audiotapes
- videotapes
- floppy disks containing multimedia presentations
- photographs of larger art work or design and technology work
- plans for design and technology work
- science reports
- certificates from performances and competitions
- awards
- journals
- grade sheets with feedback

Narrowing the Focus

I chose not to narrow this down. My criterion is that they have to find a way to get the learning samples into their portfolio; sometimes that means taking a photograph (I have a Polaroid camera and a 35mm camera available).

Barb's Ideas

The following learning samples are for 10th graders who are preparing a mathematics portfolio with an emphasis on algebra. The portfolio is designed to show growth over time. Here is my initial list of ideas of learning samples:

Brainstorming Potential Learning Samples

- unit quizzes with corrections
- unit tests with corrections
- unit review sheets, such as mind maps and study sheets

- homework samples
- significant notes
- lists of formulae
- problems with full, detailed solutions
- open-ended problems with full, detailed solutions
- photograph of a poster designed for class
- learning sample completed with a partner (e.g., Pairs Check)
- learning sample created with Base Group, following a Jigsaw activity
- goal-setting sheet, with identified work habits and math content goals and action plans
- journal entries
- learning samples related to multiple intelligences project
- midsemester examination with reflection and parent response

When I reviewed the list, I was able to choose items that are clearly focused for my particular purpose and type of portfolio. Because my students are preparing a growth portfolio, items such as the goal-setting sheet and midsemester examination are particularly important. The categories for this model will be based on the units of the course, unless students choose to organize their entries differently. Learning samples should represent students' learning across all the units in the course, which will relate to the criterion "variety of entries."

Narrowing the Focus

I've narrowed my original list to the following items that are relevant to the purpose, type, and categories of my chosen portfolio model.

- unit tests with corrections
- unit review sheets, such as mind maps and study sheets
- homework samples
- problems with full, detailed solutions
- learning sample completed with a partner (e.g., Pairs Check)
- goal-setting sheet, with identified work habits and math content goals and action plans
- midsemester examination with reflection and parent responses

PLANNER D
SELECTING LEARNING SAMPLES

Record the decisions you have made for students' selection of learning samples.

1. List the types of learning samples that might be appropriate for your students' portfolios:

_____

_____

_____

_____

_____

_____

_____

2. Who is involved in the process of learning sample selection?	3. How will you and your students select learning samples?	4. When are learning sample selections going to be made?
☐ Student	☐ Independent class time	☐ Regularly scheduled class times
☐ Teacher	☐ Class brainstorming	
☐ Peer	☐ Conferences with teacher	☐ End of units
☐ Parent or guardian	☐ Portfolio round robin	☐ Midsemester or term reporting periods
☐ Family member	☐ Partner interviews	
☐ Educational authorities (e.g., state or provincial bodies)	☐ Portfolio days	☐ End of semester or term
	☐ Conferences with others	☐ End of year
☐ _____	☐ _____	

5. What is the teacher's role in selecting learning samples?

_____

_____

_____

_____

_____

REFLECTIONS

OVERVIEW

In this chapter, you'll learn what reflection is and why it is essential to learning. Four elements of meaningful learning and cognitive development are discussed and illustrated with student samples. A range of strategies for engaging students in meaningful reflection is provided. The activities are designed to help you think about quality reflection and create concrete prompts to assist students in the reflection process. This chapter will help you plan for meaningful student reflection and facilitate implementation decisions that promote student success.

WHY REFLECTION IS ESSENTIAL

We do not learn from experience. We learn from reflecting on experience.

—John Dewey

Students produce work to show what they have gained from involvement in learning experiences. Merely collecting and storing that work in a folder, however, cuts short the potential of that collection as an effective tool for assessment and instruction. Adding an element of reflection fosters the critical thinking and decision making necessary for continuous learning and improvement. What is reflection? Reflection happens when students think about how their work meets established criteria; they analyze the effectiveness of their efforts, and plan for improvement. Reflecting on what has been learned and articulating that learning to others is the heart and soul of the portfolio process. Without reflection, a portfolio has little meaning.

Random House Webster's Dictionary (1998) defines a portfolio as "a collection of drawings, photographs, etc., representative of a person's work" (p. 557). Making thoughtful selections requires learners to make judgments about which work best represents personal accomplishments relevant to established criteria. Reflection plays an integral role in making those selections and in a learner's ability to determine courses of action that are most effective in reaching future objectives.

Essentially, reflection is linked to elements that are fundamental to meaningful learning and cognitive development:

• The development of metacognition—the capacity for students to improve their ability to think about their thinking.

• The ability to self-evaluate—the capacity for students to judge the quality of their work based on evidence and explicit criteria for the purpose of doing better work.

• The development of critical thinking, problem solving, and decision making—the capacity for students to engage in higher-level thinking skills.

• The enhancement of teacher understanding of the learner—the capacity for teachers to know and understand more about the students with whom they work.

Each element is a dimension of the reflective process and is, by itself, a compelling rationale for the emphasis on reflection. Your goal is to engage your students in the process of reflection to enhance their capabilities and to increase your awareness of them as learners.

THE DEVELOPMENT OF METACOGNITION

Metacognition is thinking about thinking. Bruning, Schraw, and Ronning (1995) define it as "knowledge people have about their own thought processes" (p. 99). These authors view metacognition as a critical element of skilled learning. When individuals have knowledge about their own thinking processes, they are better able to exercise control over the many available cognitive skills that are needed to complete a task. To accomplish a desired goal or outcome, for example, they would have to combine and coordinate the many separate pieces of information and actions required for success. Even a common task such as mailing a letter requires numerous pieces of information for success. These pieces include knowledge of where to send the letter, how to address an envelope, legibility of the address, proper postage, postal outlet locations, and how to get to those locations. Metacognition assists individuals in managing and coordinating all of

this information in order to achieve success. Similarly, student metacognition is directly related to successful achievement on learning tasks in school and is key to the effective use of portfolios.

Metacognition has two related dimensions (Brown 1980, 1987, as cited in Bruning, Schraw, & Ronning, 1995). The first is knowledge of cognition, which includes the following components:

• Knowledge about personal learning characteristics, such as knowing what factors help or hinder memory or performance in specific situations;

• Knowledge about strategies, such as using various mnemonic strategies to enhance memory, applying research strategies to obtain information, or using problem-solving strategies to make decisions; and

• Knowledge about when and why to use a particular strategy, such as knowing that mnemonics will help when you must recall information, whereas brainstorming will help when you need to explore what you already know about a topic that you wish to research.

The second dimension of metacognition is regulation of cognition which involves

• Planning as evidenced by effectively selecting strategies and appropriating resources to achieve a goal;

• Self-monitoring as evidenced by purposefully self-testing and making needed adjustments while engaged in learning tasks or performances; and

• Self-evaluating as evidenced by judging the worthiness or effectiveness of products created and processes used.

The following student reflections were written to accompany learning samples. In these examples, the teacher comments on how the student reflections reveal the evidence of metacognition, specifically, the knowledge of cognition.

Student: Imran   **Grade:** 5

Learning Sample: "Robot" research and presentation using a Literacy Circle

Student Reflection: This entry is about a story called "Men Are Different" which we read as a group. This is a science fiction story about robots. I had a special job in my group to research on robots. I chose this entry because it shows how I can explain what I found out about robots supporting it with facts from books. Also other people learned from my research and used this information in our robot debate. I learned from this entry the importance of asking other people for feedback before the real presentation. They said to speak louder and to make a bigger diagram. In this entry the target "smart" [intelligence] I used was "word" [linguistic] for writing about robots, and the supporting intelligence I used was "people" [interpersonal] when I presented to other people and asked them for their feedback. This entry was cooperative because I presented to others and they helped me by giving me feedback in terms of my presentation skills. They benefited because they got information for the debate.

In the following comments, Imran's teacher notes evidence that Imran is becoming knowledgeable about his personal learning characteristics, one feature of knowledge of cognition. Imran shows his developing understanding of what helps his performance in specific situations.

Teacher's Reflection: Imran, in his reflection on his robot research and presentation, illustrates the importance he places on sharing and learning from others in a truly cooperative manner. He states how his peers in his literacy circle group successfully assessed his presentation (using the class created assessment model) before he did the real presentation in front of the class. Not only is he aware that he learns from others, he also is aware that his peers are able to use his ideas, which he quite capably supports with facts relevant to our class debate which followed. He accurately notes how "people smarts" help support the written and spoken component of his project.

Student: Ashley   **Grade:** 10

Learning Sample: Song for trigonometry ratios—SOHCAHTOA (Sine=Opposite/Hypotenuse, etc.)

Student Reflection: I chose to write my musical intelligence song about the trigonometry unit. I decided this because it took me awhile to figure out the methods of trigonometry. Once I realized how to use the mnemonic device, SOHCAHTOA, it became easier to understand the methods of the unit. So I decided that SOHCAHTOA might be easier for people to remember if it was in a song. This song would make it easier for people with a strong musical intelligence to remember the mnemonic device. I think this is a good idea because it provides another option to help people to memorize the trigonometry steps.

In the following comments, Ashley's teacher recognizes how Ashley is becoming more knowledgeable about a particular strategy that enhances her memory, along with when and why she might use that strategy. Again, this is evidence of knowledge of cognition, one dimension of metacognition.

Teacher's Reflection: This reflection was particularly interesting for me because I had only mentioned mnemonic devices fleetingly in class. I had no idea that Ashley had grasped the concept so well and had understood so clearly how it could help her in a subject such as mathematics. Ashley knew that connecting her musical ability with the math content would help her and possibly others as well. She created a strategy that she believed would help her to learn a critical concept and she understood that this strategy would be useful for recalling that concept in an efficient manner. Ashley was able to demonstrate a lot of creativity in applying her musical intelligence to course content and was able to identify specifically how such a creative approach could be beneficial for other students.

The following student reflections illustrate regulation of cognition. In their comments, the teachers note the students' strengths in planning, monitoring, and evaluating their own work.

Student: Mike   **Grade:** 6

Learning Sample: A tessellation drawing: The Great Escape (A tessellation is a drawing with a repeating pattern)

Student Reflection: I chose this entry because I didn't think it would become good. I didn't think it would turn out this good because it initially started out as a tessellation of Teddy bears. After my failed attempt, I readjusted it to become a tiger. After a while, there were squares between every block of tiles. I decided to fill those in with broken and unbroken cages. I then felt quite satisfied with my work. I felt better, because I worked around my problem swiftly. From this entry I learned that tessellation isn't as easy as it looks and that you can let your imagination go wild with your work (sometimes).

Teacher Reflection: Reading Mike's reflection was a real revelation to me. Mike excels in and enjoys both visual arts and mathematics. The work he hands in is always meticulously done. When I first saw his tessellation I had no idea that he had done anything but follow an original idea through to completion in a systematic way. When I read the reflection I can see how he is constantly assessing and reevaluating his work as he goes along, making changes and adjustments, and problem solving in a highly creative way. I also get a strong sense of Mike's growing ability and confidence with self-evaluation. I can see that Mike's satisfaction with his work comes not just from having a pleasing final product but from the process he went through to get to it.

Student: Jenn   **Grade:** 12

Learning Sample: Introductory Letter to Portfolio

Student Reflection: I have grown as a writer through the past year because I have learnt so much. Before this year, I had a problem with not staying to the point with my essays. Yet, this year I tried the other extreme. I wrote most of my early essays right to the point. On the other hand, those were choppy so I had to change that. So then I stayed to the point, but added smoother transitions. My transitions still need work, I do admit, but I am getting closer to an *A* as we speak!

Teacher Reflection: This reflection revealed that Jenn really understood some specific strengths and weaknesses in her writing. She identified how she had improved, and in doing so described the "journey" that she took before she was able to correct a major writing problem. I liked the fact that Jenn acknowledged that she was engaged in a growth process as a writer, rather than feeling that she had nothing else to work on. Jenn revealed that she had a clear understanding of the constant evolution of the writing process. She recognized something that needed to be improved, self-monitored as she worked on that aspect of her writing, and was conscious of the fact that she must continue to self-monitor in order to grow as a writer.

Metacognitive skills are important learning outcomes because research indicates that students who have acquired metacognitive skills are better able to compensate for both low ability and insufficient information (Swanson, 1990). Research also indicates that metacognition can be learned by children as well as adults (Jacobs & Paris, 1987; Delclos & Harrington, 1991). Through the portfolio process you can teach your students how to meaningfully reflect on the work they produce and the procedures they use.

The ability to reflect on our own thinking processes allows us to take a course of action, make adjustments while enacting it, and assess the overall strategy to determine its effectiveness (Rolheiser, 1998, p. 8).

The Ability to Self-Evaluate

Self-evaluation is an important part of metacognition and is an important concept in its own right. Self-evaluation occurs when students make judgments about their achievement and react to their judgments. Students naturally judge and make decisions about the quality of their learning and react or associate feelings with their judgments—whether or not they know how to do so effectively.

Self-perceptions of success or failure, and what students believe their successes and failures are attributed to, directly affect motivation to achieve. Without instruction, students may inappropriately attach inaccurate or negative attributions to their successes and failures. Negative judgments tend to adversely affect future learning expectations and the effort that students direct toward achieving their expectations.

By systematically teaching students strategies for reflection as part of the portfolio process, you enable students to make accurate and positive self-judgments, and in turn, promote their self-confidence. Self-confidence, then, influences the future learning goals that students set and the effort they devote to accomplishing those goals. An upward cycle of learning results when students confidently set learning goals that are moderately challenging yet realistic, and then exert the effort, energy, and resources needed to accomplish those goals. Successful achievement allows positive self-judgments and self-reactions, which continues to fuel an upward cycle of learning. Effective student self-evaluation, therefore, tends to enhance student achievement (Rolheiser, 1996).

Recent studies indicate that student attitudes, effort, achievement, self-appraisal, and goal setting are enhanced when students are taught self-evaluation techniques that enable them to attribute their success to personal actions, help them to identify concrete steps for improvement, and promote their ownership for learning (Rolheiser, 1996; Ross, Rolheiser, & Hogaboam-Gray, 1998, 1999). By teaching students strategies for self-evaluation that require reflection, and by helping students learn how to systematically engage in those strategies through their portfolio work, you may enhance their success.

The following student reflections demonstrate how students are engaged in self-evaluation across grade levels. The accompanying teacher reflec-tions reveal important information that they gleaned from students' self-evaluations.

Student: Trevor **Grade:** Kindergarten
Learning Sample: Social Skills Checklist (self-evaluation)
Student Reflection: *(Prompt) I like this piece because I got better at* shareing, waiting politely. *(Prompt) I am still working on* tidying up solveing my problems.
Teacher Reflection: Trevor's reflection demonstrates his ability to self-evaluate and articulate his growth as a learner over time. He was empowered and encouraged to self-select the social skills he felt he needed to work on, and together we generated realistic strategies to meet these expectations. The sense of pride Trevor conveys when acknowledging the social skills he has learned is evident. Achieving success by reaching many of his initial goals, Trevor was more willing to tackle new goals for the future.

Student: Sanji **Grade:** 6
Learning Sample: News Broadcast—Narrative Piece of Writing
Student Reflection: My entry is the "Martian" broadcast story which I wrote based on the real science fiction broadcast "War of the Worlds" broadcast over the radio in 1938. In the real story Martians landed on earth and were beginning to take over. In my story the "Martians" which are really robots land and succeed but the police stop them. I chose this entry because it falls under the writing expectation for our portfolio and I think it is one of my best pieces that conveys a central idea using well-linked paragraphs. I learned that whenever you are writing stories you should have proper paragraphs, be descriptive and use detail, have a beginning, middle, and end and that I should always check for spelling and grammar. I used "word smarts" [linguistic intelligence] when I wrote the story and "logic smarts" [mathematical-logical intelligence] when I planned it using a web. "People smarts" [interpersonal intelligences] were used when Adam proofread it for me. I had a partner who read my story and

gave me feedback on all the areas I was good at and the areas I had to work on and it helped me. So I knew that from another person's perspective my story was good.

Teacher Reflection: Sanji, in his reflection on his narrative piece of writing, clearly indicates he is aware of the criteria he was to address by writing this piece. Both the content and structural components of narrative writing are acknowledged, showing an understanding of this form of communication. He further demonstrates this understanding by stating how he uses his personal knowledge of his "smarts" [multiple intelligences] to his advantage in each of the different steps of the writing process. This awareness of how best to use his "smarts" is the reason his final product is creative, detailed, organized in different ways, revised, and edited. His final comment indicates he is quite comfortable with a peer responding to his work to offer some constructive criticism. Sanji has learned that peers can be superb writing teachers and he can personally grow from letting them assess his work.

Student: Grant   **Grade:** 7
Learning Sample: Model, Presentation, and Brochure on Hong Kong
Student Reflection: Another well-improved skill is my interpersonal abilities, working well with others. I have on other projects done a lot of the work, not because my group was unwilling to do it but because I wanted it done my way. (If you want something done right, do it yourself!) However, this put a great work load on me. So this year I have tried to equalize the work, but not do less myself. . . . I feel I did a pretty good job and put a lot of effort into the project, a study of southeast Asia. We (Mike, Brandon and I) chose to do Hong Kong as a model and brochure. I think I helped to improve my interpersonal skills. I did my part and made sure everyone else did, too.
Teacher Reflection: In this reflection I can see Grant's increasing ability not only to self-evaluate his performance on a particular piece of work, but his ability to

reflect on himself as a learner over time. I can see him assessing himself on a goal which he had set for himself a few months earlier, which was to develop his interpersonal and leadership skills. As I read the reflection I sense that Grant's confidence in his ability to work with others is increasing and that he is able to view his own efforts in a very positive light. I think this is really important. I think students, particularly at this age level, frequently have difficulty self-assessing in positive or constructive ways. But here we can see Grant clearly recognizes the positive steps he has taken and recognizes his own growth.

Student: Stephanie   **Grade:** 12
Learning Sample: Letter of Introduction to Portfolio
Student Reflection: In the beginning of the course the class was asked to write a self evaluation of our own strengths, weaknesses and views of the [previous] English course. After reading that evaluation, I can see that I have made improvements in all areas. Gradually I have overcome my awful habit of procrastination and one of the essays this year was completed over a week ahead of the due date. Although I have improved in these areas, I can still continue growing as a writer and work harder to achieve success.
Teacher Reflection: Stephanie's reflection reveals the importance of completing a self-evaluation early in a course and then revisiting it toward the end of that particular learning process. By doing this, Stephanie now has the satisfaction of recognizing formally that she has improved in all key areas of concern and, in particular, identifies a problem of procrastination that she was able to overcome in a significant way. Stephanie also acknowledges that while she has improved in some areas, she can still continue to grow; she understands that hard work is a critical component of that entire process. What I value most about this reflection is that Stephanie recognized and affirmed her own improvement, which is far more meaningful for her development as a writer and as a person than being given external praise for her accomplishments.

CRITICAL THINKING, PROBLEM SOLVING, AND DECISION MAKING

Reflection is inherent in thinking critically, solving problems, and making decisions. Learners who effectively use thinking skills must be able to identify and define problems and issues, select and implement appropriate strategies, and monitor and adjust courses of action. Students tend to experience greater success with thinking skills when they are explicitly aware of the sequence of steps required to effectively use those thinking skills.

Bruning, Schraw, and Ronning (1995) discuss four levels of awareness from Swartz and Perkins (1990). At the *tacit* level, you are able to use a thinking skill, but do so without awareness. At the *awareness* level, you know you are using the thinking skill but cannot explain it. At the *strategic* level, you are consciously aware of the thinking skill and use your knowledge of it to regulate its use. At the *reflective* level, you understand how the thinking skill works, can explain it to others, can reflect on the skill in relationship to desired goals and outcomes, and then use it strategically for those purposes. Teaching students explicit procedures and strategies for reflection in the portfolio process helps them to become better thinkers by guiding them toward reflective use of thinking skills.

In the array of student reflections shown below, there is diverse evidence of students developing critical thinking, problem-solving, and decision-making skills. The teachers gained insight into their students' developing skills by reading their portfolio reflections. Without the student reflections, evidence of student development might not have been available to these teachers.

Student: Tiffany   **Grade:** Kindergarten
Learning Sample: Printmaking of a Color Pattern (e.g., red, yellow, green, red, yellow, green)
Student Reflection: I don't like this piece because it is rag [wrong] because I wsnt thingking!

Teacher Reflection: Tiffany's reflection clearly conveyed her appreciation that this patterning sample was not an example of her best work. In fact, it was a pattern "gone wrong" and Tiffany recognized this. She was able to critically think about her work and demonstrated an awareness of her own abilities. Tiffany identified a "thinking" component as being an essential tool for learning and valued its merits in affecting her performance. This was an important revelation for me as her teacher. A bright child, Tiffany delighted in the social aspects of the Kindergarten program. However, she displayed a certain reluctance to perform teacher-directed activities. Learning that Tiffany had acquired age-appropriate metacognitive skills allowed me to work with her in setting goals for future performances. The results were inspiring. Tiffany went on to demonstrate tremendous growth in the depth of her reflections over the course of the year, as well as enhanced academic achievement.

Student: Mike   **Grade:** 6
Learning Sample: Creation of a Math Game
Student Reflection: This entry is about how I made my game with the minimum requirements of a few pizza tables. If I had the proper tools, material and ample time I would've done this much better but I had to improvise. I think I did a good job, though, but I have yet to receive my mark. I did this solo because I already had plans for my project. I think I did do a good job on the icons (or player pieces). I liked how my creativity shows in this game.

Teacher Reflection: When I read this reflection I get a sense that Mike was not entirely satisfied with this piece of work. Yet he is able to look at it and identify the elements of it that were successful for him. I think, too, he identifies what did hold him back from his best work without making excuses. It's clear from the entry that Mike doesn't need a mark or the teacher's judgment to help him decide whether he likes his work or whether he has done a "good job." He knew he wanted his pizza game to go into his portfolio well before he received his mark. It tells me that Mike is someone who

wants to put forward his best effort and recognizes where his strengths are.

His reflection also makes me consider the situation I set up for the students in this particular exercise. Did restricting the time and materials push their creativity, was having to improvise a good experience, or was it frustrating? Would more time have helped some students, such as Mike, achieve more and feel more satisfied with their work? Or, was this an authentic experience that helped some students begin to accept what they can do in limited situations and encourage them to be creative in different ways?

Student: Shannon   **Grade:** 10

Learning Sample: Textbook Work, The Equation of a Line

Student Reflection: I entered this piece of work because it is something that I learned from and improved upon.

When this work was taught, I didn't quite understand how to do it. I soon realized that by applying common knowledge, e.g., the area of a triangle, and theory's taught in co-ordinate geometry, I could easily find small, quick steps to finding out the answer. Therefore, I learned that by just thinking and applying math steps already taught, I could put together easy steps and do the math quite quickly and precisely.

Teacher Reflection: Shannon revealed here that she understood that she needed to apply previous knowledge to a problem and to break that problem down into a series of steps before she could solve it. These are critically important skills for learning mathematics. Too often students are overwhelmed by the complexity of a problem and they give up rather than trying to analyze that problem and see what information is required to solve it. Shannon was not always patient with herself when she encountered tough material, and so this was particularly meaningful because she did not give up—she applied appropriate thinking skills, solved the problem and, equally importantly, she acknowledged that she could do this in the future for other mathematical problems.

TEACHER UNDERSTANDING OF THE LEARNER

Students' reflections on work reveal their perceptions of how well they are doing. Knowing students' perceptions is invaluable for a teacher because they provide information on the sophistication of students' thinking about the criteria for achievement—and on how accurately students are applying the criteria. Student reflection can reveal other valued aspects of learning that are not readily apparent and, therefore, go unnoticed and remain hidden.

Rather than only collecting learning samples, asking students to articulate reflections on their work (either orally or in writing) provides a clearer and fuller picture of each student as a learner. A reflection may reveal, for example, that a student chose a piece of work for the portfolio not because it is the highest quality finished product, but because it shows persistence in exerting effort toward an especially challenging task. In other words, through the student's reflection, the teacher learns that the student is proud of the personal effort put forth to produce the work, realizes that the task would not have been completed without sustained effort, and shows a new awareness of the personal capacity to persist in learning tasks.

The following story about a young photographer and his mentor illustrates how involving students in reflection can provide teachers with hidden insights:

Every year the aspiring photographer brought a stack of his best prints to an old, honored photographer, seeking his judgment. Every year the old man studied the prints and painstakingly ordered them into two piles, bad and good. Every year the old man moved a certain landscape print into the bad stack. At length he turned to the young man: "You submit this same landscape every year, and every year I put it on the bad stack. Why do you like it so much?" The young photographer said, "Because I had to climb a mountain to get it." (Dillard, 1989, p. 6).

Teachers can deepen their understanding of the learners with whom they work by reading their portfolio reflections and valuing the information revealed by them. The following examples from different grades provide a brief snapshot of the kinds of treasures that teachers may discover in their students' reflections.

Student: Haseeb   **Grade:** Kindergarten
Learning Sample: Tissue Paper Apple (artwork)
Student Reflection: I don't like it beucse I wored hard on my apple. I don't like to work hard.
Teacher Reflection: I could not have been more surprised when I read Haseeb's reflection. As a Senior Kindergarten student and English as a Second Language learner, Haseeb tackled all assigned tasks confidently and with care. He rarely expressed emotion in response to his work or play experiences and never gave me any verbal indication that he was at all feeling pressured to perform. I was curious about Haseeb's choice of words for this particular piece of work, as it merely involved cutting, gluing, and crumpling tissue paper. It has been my experience that most Kindergarten children view activities that incorporate a written component to be "work" and all others to be "play." This did not seem to be the case with Haseeb. He did not appear to experience any undo frustration while completing tasks involving small hand muscle skills and was a proficient and prolific writer. Without any visible or audible signs of displeasure, modifying Haseeb's program so as not to turn him off learning became my challenge. I found that encouraging him to do his best work and helping him to reflect on both the process and the products he created were beneficial in keeping him motivated and excited about his observable growth.

Student: Ryan   **Grade:** 2
Learning Sample: Viewing a video on penguins and then writing a story about what students learned.
Student Reflection: *(Prompt) Why did you choose to put this piece in your portfolio?* It's because it is very special to me. It's because it took me a long time to finish it.
Teacher Reflection: In reading Ryan's reflection, I was inspired by his valuing of the process and the effort he put forth, rather than the finished product itself. Intellectually, Ryan is an extremely capable child. Unfortunately, he is hampered by weak small hand muscles and consequently the legibility of his work is often cause for concern. Ryan's personal frustration with his "messy" printing often leads to difficulties rereading his work or play a role in his decision to just write less. This video reflection clearly told me that Ryan is tremendously proud of his work. His ability to persevere with his assigned task for a prolonged period of time, despite his printing impediment, showed me that Ryan is capable of producing quality work with extreme effort. This reflection allowed me to better understand Ryan's needs as a learner and to ensure that all his sustained written efforts are rewarded with praise and encouragement to promote further success.

Student: Hanieh   **Grade:** 9
Learning Sample: Mathography—An autobiography in math
Student Reflection: I have allot of self-confident in doing my homework independently, writing unit tests, and grasping new concepts now than I had before. I don't really understand the new way that we have to solve problems. I mean that I don't understand the sheet we always receive whenever a problem is given to us and we are suppose to solve it one step at a time.

I think my ability to do mathematics has really improved since before. I understand concepts more clearly and feel more confident about learning. I have really improved my learning skills in working with a group, organizing my notebook and studying for tests and exams.

Things that I really enjoyed doing in this class was the Inside-Outside Circle and going to the computer lab and playing that game. I don't think I really hated anything we have done. In my opinion this has been a great and rather fun class.

Teacher Reflection: This reflection revealed a great deal about the learner, particularly because this student was a quiet girl who rarely chose to speak out in class. Through this type of final portfolio reflection I learn a lot about students, especially those who are quieter. Some things I knew about Hanieh, but other things I did not. I was glad to learn that she felt that her overall confidence had increased, and at the same time realized that I had not been totally successful in helping her to understand the problem-solving process that we had been practicing in class. Hanieh identified specific skills that she felt she had improved, which was important. I was surprised at the items that she mentioned that she enjoyed; without this type of written reflection I would never have realized that she liked the more social activities that we engaged in during the course. Finally, it was gratifying to read that Hanieh enjoyed math; positive feedback is also important for the teacher.

HOW TO ENGAGE LEARNERS IN REFLECTION

Whether the learner is a kindergarten child reflecting on a painting just completed, or an adult reflecting on the effectiveness of teamwork skills used in a cooperative task just completed, the process of reflection allows both the child and the adult to identify what worked well and what needs adjustment. To increase the likelihood that reflection will be beneficial, strategies for reflection can be directly taught and practiced. Learners who know how to engage in meaningful reflection can do so at their own initiative. To reflect meaningfully, however, requires a set of behaviors and skills. Even those who are skilled in reflection can benefit from prompts and cues that motivate deeper levels of thinking. Here are some ways teachers can facilitate this process:

Define what reflection is and why it is important for learners and their learning. As discovered in a study examining students' attitudes toward self-evaluation, limited or no understanding of reflective processes may impede learners' willingness to engage in that process and may create unnecessary barriers (Ross, Rolheiser. & Hogaboam-Gray, 2000). One way of decreasing these problems is to provide a simple, clear definition of reflection and the reasons it is relevant to students and their learning. For example, share the following definition with your students:

> Reflection: Ideas or conclusions that are a result of your thinking about your work. These ideas are connected to specific criteria and may help you determine future goals and actions.

Then, invite students to generate words or images that come to mind when they think about reflection. You may then create a brainstorming list or mind map to launch into a discussion about why reflection is important. Before the discussion, prepare a few reasons to help start the discussion. For example, if you teach high school, emphasize the value of students independently identifying strengths and weaknesses in their work; over time, the goal would be for students to apply this reflective skill to other areas of their lives. If you teach elementary school, you might highlight the importance of a student sharing work that demonstrates her best effort with others. Reflection, at an age-appropriate level, is a way for students to provide you with additional information about their learning.

Model the reflection process for students. Much of what we learn is through modeling. This concept is an integral part of effective teaching, and is used in many instructional approaches (e.g., direct instruction model). Albert Bandura's (1977) social learning theory and work in behavioral modeling has contributed to our understanding that many human behaviors are learned through observations. "From observing others one forms an idea of how new behaviors are formed, and on later occasions this coded information serves as a guide for action" (Bandura, 1977, p. 22).

Because the most critical and distinctive component of a portfolio is the reflective component, students need opportunities to observe others, especially teachers, model new reflective skills. The information students glean from observations serves as a guide for their own reflective actions. Although modeling can occur in many ways, it's easy to start with one of the following ideas.

• Choose a meaningful artifact from your professional or personal life and share both the artifact and your written reflection with the students. During this sharing, ask students to identify the important features of the reflection.

• Choose two anonymous short reflections written by former students or students from another class. Have students compare and contrast these reflections to tease out the characteristics of higher-quality reflections.

• Choose a weak reflective sample and have the class brainstorm ways to make it a stronger reflection.

• Choose work samples and regularly practice oral reflection as a whole class, identifying the strengths and weaknesses of the samples.

• Select a common learning experience and have all students write a reflection, using the following sample prompts to guide their writing:

– Describe this experience in your own words.

– What part of this experience did you like the most?

– Complete the following statement: Now I understand . . .

As you model for students, remember the key principles: (1) effective demonstrations require teachers to accurately model all the behaviors that they wish the students to later demonstrate, (2) students need to be aware of what to focus on in the modeling, and (3) discussion and elaboration during the demonstration enhances subsequent student performance (Arends, 1994). One way to help ensure that you and your students continue to improve in the reflection process is to begin a chart that lists the attributes of effective reflection. The list will grow and deepen as you take students through various modeling experiences. Also, show students how to connect their reflections to the goals, purposes, and criteria established for the portfolio.

3. Provide starting points to build success in reflection. The beginning processes of reflection need to have sufficient structure for learners to experience success. For example, a kindergarten teacher might offer three icons and ask students to choose the one that best reflects how they feel about a given piece of work (e.g., a happy face, neutral face, or sad face). See **Figure 5.1** for a sample worksheet. For young children, building success might mean providing lots of practice with verbal prompts and verbal responses regarding aspects of their work. You might ask a student who has completed a science experiment, "What was the most important thing that you learned from doing this experiment?" Oral practice can be followed by the teacher or the student recording the responses, depending on the student's abilities. The key is using a focused prompt. Older students might be given a structured set of prompts for each assignment or a variety of prompts to choose from for a particular entry. **Figure 5.2** is an example of how you can offer young students a worksheet to prompt their reflections on particular assignments. You may wish to vary the prompts according to the objective of the assignment. For example, at the end of a math unit, students might be given several possibilities: "I am very proud of this work because . . .", "What I learned from doing this piece was . . .", or "This piece was a challenge for me because . . .". See **Figure 5.3** (pp. 44–45) for several suggested

FIGURE 5.1

Portfolio Reflection Sheet for
Young Students

For young students, a simple worksheet with graphics is a good way to introduce and prompt reflection.

1. When I look at my work I feel

2. From my work, you can tell that I am good at

_____

_____

_____

_____

_____

3. I would like to get better at

_____

_____

_____

_____

_____

_____

(adapted from Schwartz, 1996, workshop handout)

FIGURE 5.2

Portfolio Reflection Worksheet

Offer young students a worksheet similar to this one to prompt their reflections on particular assignments. You may wish to vary the prompts offered according to the objective of the assignment.

Name _____   Date of Learning Sample _____

Entry Title _____   Entry Date_____

Focus: Identify the category for this portfolio entry: _____

_____

Describe your entry. You may use the following prompts.

• What is your entry about?

• Why did you choose this as an entry?

• What did you learn?

• How, did you grow or change?

_____

_____

_____

_____

_____

_____

_____

_____

_____

_____

_____

_____

43

FIGURE 5.3

Short Reflection Prompts

Use this worksheet with students who need structure in reflecting on their work. Half sheets may motivate students who either perceive a task as "easy" when the questions don't take up a whole page or who perceive a whole page to be overwhelming.

I am very proud of this work because _____
_____
_____
_____
_____
_____
_____

Signed _____ Date _____

What I learned from doing this piece was _____
_____
_____
_____
_____
_____
_____

Signed _____ Date _____

This piece was a challenge for me because _____
_____
_____
_____
_____
_____
_____

Signed _____ Date _____

FIGURE 5.3 (continued)

This piece shows that I understand how to _____

_____

_____

_____

_____

_____

_____

Signed _____ Date _____

This piece is important because _____

_____

_____

_____

_____

_____

_____

Signed _____ Date _____

I think my parents will be impressed with this work because _____

_____

_____

_____

_____

_____

_____

Signed _____ Date _____

reflection prompts you can offer students who need structure in reflecting on their work. Half sheets may motivate students who either perceive a task to be easy when the questions don't fill a whole page or who are overwhelmed by being given a whole page to complete.

Help students move from general reflections to criteria-specific reflections. As students begin the reflection process, their initial attempts are likely to be vague or general (Bennett, Rolheiser, & Stevahn, 1991). You will want to move your students toward more analytic and specific reflections. Here are some ideas that may help you to encourage students' growth on the reflective continuum:

• Probe for clarification in responding to students' initial efforts. For example, if a student writes, "I like this piece of work because we cooperated on it," you might respond, "Specifically, what did you do in producing this piece of work that shows cooperation?"

• Model the procedure for reflection, using phrases that are specific in describing actions. For example, students might reflect on their participation in a group activity by starting with "An action I took that I think helped our group be successful was . . ." The specific ending to that response might be " . . . by collecting the materials needed," or " . . . by keeping track of the time," or " . . . helping our group stick to the task."

• Provide sentence starters that demand higher levels of reflective thinking or that demand specificity for completion. For example, the starter "This piece of work compares to my last piece in the following ways . . ." encourages analytical thinking. The starter "I really helped my teammates when I . . ." encourages specific reflection related to a cooperative learning experience.

• Encourage coaching and feedback to deepen learners' capacity for reflection over time.

A framework that teachers have found helpful in assisting students to move toward specific reflections is a framework called The 3 Rs: Retell, Relate, Reflect (Schwartz & Bone, 1995), as outlined in **Figure 5.4.** Students can be introduced to the framework as a guide for deepening the reflections attached to their learning samples.

Provide regular opportunities to practice reflection. The capacity for reflection improves with practice. Students need regular opportunities to reflect on their work, both orally and in writing. If reflections are done only at the end of the portfolio process, your students may not achieve the quality and depth of reflection that is possible when they practice over time using the ideas discussed in this chapter.

Activity 6 and **Activity 7** are designed to help you consolidate your thoughts about the process of reflection. You may want to complete both activities or just the one that best meets your needs. **Figure 5.5** shows how Barb and Carol worked through **Activity 6**, including their PMI chart for samples from **Appendix C** and their summary of key attributes of good reflection.

GROUNDWORK FOR REFLECTION

Helping students build their ability to reflect on their work is a long-term proposition. Although your ideas and processes for supporting their reflection are likely to change over time, it is important to think about how you present and model reflection for your students. Use **Planner E** to establish the groundwork for reflection in your classroom. As you and your students proceed with reflection, you'll need to give them opportunities for practice and ongoing support as they develop skills.

Students develop skills as they create individual reflections on learning samples and also as they write an introductory letter to the portfolio. In the introductory letter, students pull together their thoughts on the portfolio, and it is likely to be the last reflective piece placed in the portfolio. As your

FIGURE 5.4

Retell, Relate, Reflect

One framework that seems to assist students in moving to specific reflections is "The 3 Rs: Retell, Relate, Reflect," (Schwartz & Bone, 1995). Students can be introduced to the framework as a guide for deepening their learning sample reflections.

Retell Retell in your own words Summarize the information State the main idea List the sequence of ideas Point out details Describe significant parts Answer specific parts Clarify information	**Related prompts may include** This was about . . . I noticed that . . . The most significant part was . . . A thought I especially liked was . . . I particularly liked, valued, or enjoyed . . . An idea that captured my interest was . . . Key words for me were . . . An idea that "sparkled" for me was . . .
Relate Make connections Refer to personal experiences, books, media, issues, events, related topics, feelings Compare Contrast Analyze Give examples	**Related prompts may include** This reminds me of . . . This makes me think of . . . Something I identify with is . . . It makes me feel . . . What I found especially meaningful or significant for me was . . .
Reflect Draw conclusions beyond the text or situation Apply judgment State opinions Share insights and new understandings Ask relevant questions Give reasons for what you did	**Related prompts may include** Now I understand that . . . I think that . . . I wonder why or if . . . I realize now that . . . How . . . ? A question raised in my mind is . . . Maybe . . . Something that you wrote that pushed my own thinking was . . . I learned that you . . . Thank you for reminding me how important it is to . . . An idea that "sparkled" for me was . . . because . . .

(adapted with permission from Schwartz, 1995)

ACTIVITY 6
Reflecting on Reflection

Use this activity to think about quality of reflection by identifying strengths and weaknesses in a variety of student reflections. Sample reflections are provided in **Appendix C**.

To do this activity, you'll also need **Figure 5.5, Appendix B, Appendix C**, and a pen. Use this activity with a large group or modify it to fit your situation.

1. From a larger group, participants should gather into groups of four.
2. In the group of four, subdivide into partnerships of two. Each partnership should select two different student reflection samples from those provided in **Appendix C** (each group of four should select four different sample reflections).
3. Each partnership collaborates on completing the PMI Chart (**Appendix B**) for both samples. If anyone needs guidance in filling out the chart, see **Figure 5.5.** (The PMI Chart is designed so that each sample is examined separately.)
4. Partnerships return to their groups of four and share information and observations about the samples. As a group, the participants record the attributes that best portray high-quality reflection (blank attributes chart is at the end of **Appendix B**).
5. As a whole group, participants can learn from each other by discussing and sharing characteristics that are common to high-quality reflections.

students organize their portfolios for a final viewing or sharing, they benefit from focusing on the key features of organization and substance that they want to highlight in their introduction. Writing the letter is a rich opportunity for students to develop analytical skills.

You may need to provide writing prompts or a general framework for younger students and those who are new to the portfolio process. The introductory letter is the first item in a portfolio and should be a polished piece of writing that is attractively presented. The letter also provides the student with the opportunity to make a personal connection with the viewer. Sample formats and guidelines, along with some samples of student letters of introduction, are provided in Chapter 6.

ACTIVITY 7
Generating Prompts for Reflection

Use this group activity to generate a range of writing prompts
to assist students in improving the quality of their reflections.
The following materials are suggested: masking tape, flip chart
paper (one per group of four participants), and a felt marker
and pen for each person.

1. Gather into small groups of four colleagues who teach the same or
similar grades.

2. Using a roundtable cooperative format, pass a flip chart sheet systemati-
cally around the table. Each person writes an idea and passes the paper to
the next person. Continue passing the sheet until each person generates at
least three ideas. Your ideas should be focused on the following question:
What written or oral prompts would support your students in reflection?
Examples
- This portfolio item is important to me because . . .
- If I could do this work over again I would . . .
- Something important I learned from doing this activity is . . .

3. Post your flip chart for other groups to view.

4. Walk around to review the charts and record your favorite prompts.

FIGURE 5.5

PMI Response to Activity 6 (Reflecting on Reflection)

To analyze the effectiveness of a student's reflection, you can measure the results in a PMI chart. The example below shows how Barb and Carol worked through **Activity 6**, first identifying important components of the sample reflections and then synthesizing those ideas into the attributes chart. Refer to **Appendix C** for the student samples they analyzed. Use the blank template in **Appendix B** to create your own PMI chart.

Attributes Recording Chart

Plus	Minus	Interesting
Sample #3: Mike • He identified what the entry is about • He says why he chose the particular learning sample	• No elaboration of what was learned • No learning process is outlined • He didn't identify specific strengths or weaknesses	• There's a refreshing directness of tone!
Sample #4: Sarah • She identified what the entry is about • She stated why she chose the entry with specific reasons for her choice • She described learning processes that helped her • She identified strategies that will help her to be successful in the future	• What was identified as a "lesson learned" was not applied to the reflection itself (e.g., check spelling and grammar) • She could have elaborated more on how the characters in the picture helped her create her story	• Recognition of Sarah's effort is important to her

Attributes of Successful Student Reflections

Barb and Carol identified the following attributes as best portraying high-quality reflections based on their analysis and discussion of two student samples.

• A short retelling of what the learning sample is

• An explanation of why the entry is chosen, accompanied by specific reasons

• The learning processes are identified and elaborated upon

• Specific strengths and weaknesses are acknowledged and explained

• Specific strategies or goals are identified to promote future growth

PLANNER E
REFINING THE REFLECTIVE PROCESS

As with the implementation of any new process, the implementation of portfolios in your classroom or school will prompt questions. Prepare yourself for stakeholders' questions by thinking about your best answers to these questions.

1. How will you define reflection with your students?

_____

_____

_____

_____

2. If a parent asks why your students are doing reflections, what reasons would you give?

_____

_____

_____

_____

3. What ways of modeling reflection will you use with your students?

_____

_____

_____

_____

4. How will you initially engage your learners in the reflective process? Over time, how will you deepen this process?

_____

_____

_____

_____

STORING AND ORGANIZING PORTFOLIOS

6

OVERVIEW

This chapter contains many practical suggestions for storing and organizing your students' portfolios. The constraints and realities of your particular setting will influence your decisions about portfolio storage. Portfolio storage is an important part of organizing and keeping track of learning samples and completed entries and it requires students to use appropriate organizational skills. **Activity 8** helps you make key decisions about ongoing storage of students' work. Because most portfolios need to be prepared and organized for sharing with others (as discussed in Chapter 7), you'll find an outline for an organizational component that can help students consolidate their thinking about their portfolios. Often, this consolidation becomes an introduction to the portfolio. **Planner F** provides a place for you to record key ideas for ensuring manageability of the entire portfolio process.

STORING LEARNING SAMPLES AND ENTRIES

Storing learning samples and portfolio entries involves two major considerations: the type of container for the entries and the storing of those containers. Because classroom space is always at a premium, you need to be realistic and creative about what will work for you. Here are some variables you will want to consider:

- purpose and type of portfolio
- nature of the learning samples (e.g., size, shape)
- durability of containers
- size of containers
- age of students
- shelf or cupboard space
- ease of access and frequency of access needed
- accessibility (public or private)
- price and availability

CHOOSING PORTFOLIO STORAGE CONTAINERS

Consider the variables unique to your setting before deciding on the best container for your students' portfolios. The following containers have been used successfully for the portfolios of students at various levels:

- pizza boxes
- letter-size folders with pockets
- legal-size file folders with stapled sides
- plastic tote boxes with lids
- folders created from heavy cardboard, stapled up the sides
- laundry detergent boxes
- cereal boxes
- computer disks
- hanging file folders
- binders (with clear plastic pockets, pocket folders, or dividers)
- accordion files

FINDING STORAGE SPACE

Once you have identified appropriate containers, you will know how much space is required for the storage of the portfolios. If privacy and protection is an issue, portfolios may need to be kept in locked cupboards or filing cabinets. Otherwise, storage space is all that is necessary. Use **Activity 8** to start thinking about storage space for your students' portfolios. **Figure 6.1** shows an example of how one teacher worked through the portfolio storage needs of her class.

TRACKING ENTRIES

Keeping track of entries, along with the information relevant to those entries (e.g., date of entry, related categories or outcomes, and peer responses) is a key dimension of the portfolio process. Tracking entries helps students to organize and monitor their work and provides a snapshot of the portfolio process. For example, a quick look at a tracking sheet or a working table of contents may reveal information about regularity of entries, balance of entries across categories, and frequency of peer responses. A tracking process that works effectively is the use of a table of contents.

TABLE OF CONTENTS

A chronological table of contents is one way students can track their entries. As the student completes each entry, information about it is recorded on a working table of contents. The information should include the date and focus or title of each entry. Optional information might include names of peers who respond to the entry and a place for the teacher to indicate if the entry has been reviewed or evaluated. The advantage of a working table of contents is that it can change, hence students feel relaxed and not locked into particular entries for the final portfolio.

How many entries constitute a final portfolio is determined by the purpose and type of that portfolio. For example, if the purpose of the collection of work is to demonstrate growth in literacy throughout the 8th grade, the number of entries must be sufficient to reflect all types of literature

---

**ACTIVITY 8
IDEAS for Storing Students' Portfolios**

Use the following steps to help you make key decisions about portfolio storage in your classroom. If you want ideas on how proceed, see **Figure 6.1** for a sample response.

Index the facts as you see them.
Define the problem.
Expand on ideas or possible alternatives.
Adopt a criterion or criteria.
Select and sell your ideas to others.

(adapted from Bellanca, 1992)

FIGURE 6.1

Sample Response to Activity 8 (Storing Students' Portfolios)

The following is an example of how one teacher considered several aspects of collecting, protecting, and accessing students' materials for portfolios. The factors that you consider as you complete **Activity 8** may be similar to the ones below.

Index the facts
- storage space in the classroom is available, but limited
- containers should be visible and readily available (in the classroom)
- containers need to hold a fair amount of work because our portfolios are cross-curricular
- containers can serve to help students in organizing their work
- containers should not be a big expense for students
- containers need to hold a variety of work
- containers need to be sturdy because students will carry them between home and school
- portfolios will go with students from grade to grade

Define the problem
- I need sturdy portfolio containers that can hold a variety of work and help students keep their work organized and protected.

Expand on ideas or possible alternatives
- Possible containers: pizza boxes, cereal boxes, detergent boxes, three-ring binders, tote boxes

Adopt criteria
- sturdy
- inexpensive
- aid organization
- hold a variety of materials
- easy to store in limited space
- easy to transport

Select and Sell your ideas to others

Although pizza boxes, cereal boxes, and detergent boxes are sturdy and inexpensive, they don't provide an easy way for students to organize and maintain their work. Boxes can become tattered and may be difficult to store because of their unusual and inconsistent sizes.

Tote boxes provide superior protection, but again do not help students organize their work. Tote boxes are attractive and easy to store and stack, but they can take up considerable space and can be clumsy to carry to and from school.

Three-ring binders can help students organize their work and offer a familiar organizing system. For example, students can punch holes in their work, or use plastic sleeves, and place it in the binder where it can be organized with dividers or tabs. Binders can be stored easily on most bookshelves and fit in most file or tote boxes. They are easy to transport and protect the work inside. While there is a cost associated with binders, it is not exorbitant and often gently used binders can be found.

and creative writing covered in that particular curriculum. If the purpose of the portfolio is to highlight best work in an 11th grade mathematics unit, however, the number of entries would likely be fewer. Portfolios that represent learning over an extended period of time (e.g., a semester or full year) often contain five to ten entries, with each entry including the learning samples, reflection sheets, and responses to the entry.

When students are preparing to organize the contents of the portfolio for final review, the working table of contents yields the information they need for the final table of contents. The final table of contents represents the chosen subset of entries and does not have to be chronological. Some students, for example, may want their best work as a lead for their portfolios. Others may discover themes around which to organize the entries or their teacher may provide guidelines or suggestions for organization. Some teachers find it helpful to have students record the working table of contents on one side of a sheet of paper with the final version on the other side.

INTRODUCING THE PORTFOLIO TO OTHERS

Along with the final table of contents, a useful part of many portfolios is a polished introductory piece, such as a visual organizer or a letter of introduction. The introduction allows the learner to communicate important information to the audience and includes relevant information about the learner and the classroom setting. The student might include a description of how the portfolio is organized, personal strengths and weaknesses, advantages and disadvantages of the portfolio process, and a self-evaluation of learning along with future goals and action plans. Depending on the age and skill level of the learner, the teacher may choose to structure the introductory piece.

Although the following suggestions for introductions to portfolios are specifically targeted to meet the needs of elementary, middle, or high school learners, you can modify them to meet the level of your students.

Graphic organizers. Students can create a graphic representation to reveal key aspects of themselves as individuals and learners. This method of introduction might include pictures, drawings, cut-outs, or mind maps that students create to communicate important information about themselves, such as interests, strengths, age, likes, and dislikes.

Fill-in-the-blank worksheets. Offering beginning portfolio users a structured format for an introductory letter helps them get organized. **Figure 6.2** illustrates how Sarah, a 6th grade student, introduces her portfolio to others using a structured format (see **Appendix D** for a blank template).

Introductory letters. Having students write introductory letters for their portfolios engages them in a powerful organizational process. Students write the letter of introduction at the end of the portfolio process, just before the portfolio is viewed or evaluated. The introductory piece is addressed to the potential audiences and must be proofread and error-free because it is the basis for a viewer's first impression of the portfolio. Students should be given sufficient time and support to complete this activity. You can support students by asking them to respond to the following prompts and to organize their ideas into paragraphs:

• Explain what your portfolio is about, assuming that your viewers are not familiar with portfolios.

• Describe how your entries are organized in the portfolio (e.g., chronologically, best work first, rough drafts first) and give reasons for your method of organization.

FIGURE 6.2

Sample Fill-in-the-Blank Introductory Letter

The following is a sample introductory letter from Sarah, a 6th grader. Sarah used the fill-in-the-blank structured format to introduce her portfolio. The student's spelling and grammar have been preserved. See **Appendix D** for a blank template.

An Introduction to My Portfolio

Date: <u>6/9/98</u>
My name is <u>Sarah</u>.
I am in 6th grade at <u>C.S.P. School.</u>
My teacher's name is <u>Mrs. H.</u>

- My portfolio is organized <u>topic wise. I have entries from every subject. I don't have a lot of entries from the same subject.</u>
- My portfolio shows <u>I am a person with a lot of skills and that I take time to work on my portfolio.</u>
- My best piece of work is <u>Ideal Society.</u>
- My favorite piece of work is <u>Ideal Society.</u>
- The piece that shows my best effort is <u>Romeo and Juliet (news report).</u>
- I want you to notice <u>the variety of subjects & different peers that have responded to my entries.</u>
- I think I have grown in <u>having confidence to ask different people for doing my responses.</u>
- Next year I plan to work on <u>putting only the entries that are important and right a more thoughtful reflection for them.</u>

Signature: _____

- Describe your favorite entry and explain your choice.
- Describe what you liked about creating a portfolio of your work and give reasons for your opinion.
- Describe what you found challenging about creating your portfolio and substantiate your opinion.
- Identify whether you have reached your goals. Identify future goals. Describe actions you plan to take to reach those goals.

Figure 6.3 is a letter of introduction to Lyra's 9th grade math portfolio. It shows how useful the preceding guidelines can be in helping students organize and present their portfolios to others.

After making the decisions about portfolio storage and organization, keep track of your thoughts on **Planner F**, Storing and Organizing Portfolios.

As you work through your decisions, keep in mind that the goal for choosing appropriate storage containers is to facilitate the collection and organization of the students' work. In fact, the storage containers become the initial step in organizing the portfolios as learning samples and partly finished entries are collected and stored. As students delve into those containers and become more familiar with their work and reflect on it, they shape selections into portfolio entries, setting the stage for sharing their learning with peers, parents, and other audiences.

FIGURE 6.3

Sample Letter of Introduction

The following is a sample letter of introduction written by Lyra, a 9th grader. The sample shows how Lyra used the guidelines in organizing and presenting her portfolio to others. Her spelling and grammar have been preserved.

This portfolio is a collection of math work done since the beginning of my grade nine mathematics class with Ms. Bower. It is organized from my earlier work to my most recent math work/activities. I organized it this way because I think it shows a good progression of my work and demonstrates the order in which we learned the math work. My favorite item in my portfolio is the mid-term exam. It is my favorite item because it shows good examples of all the work we had completed up to the time of the mid-term. I also like it because I got a good mark on it, which was consistent with my grade at that point. It also shows some mistakes, which I corrected and tried to learn from. I liked doing this portfolio for many reasons. It really makes you aware of what you are doing and it is a good way to motivate yourself towards good results and improving your skills. It is also nice to look over at the end of the semester and feel proud about all the work you did during the course, and see how you have changed and improved during the semester. Overall, I think it is a good, fun and interesting project that is beneficial to the mathematics class.

As I look back on my goal-setting sheet I completed in April, I am not surprised that my goals were accurate with what I need to improve or aim for. I reached my work habits goals, in correcting my work and checking answers, although I should've checked them more consistently in my daily work and specifically, my test reviews. I don't think I completed my math content goal enough, because I never involved my parents and I didn't really study, except for the mid-term exam. I usually just reviewed my work, mostly because I felt I knew the material. However, I learned after I didn't get a result on a test that was up to my standard or potential. That experience taught me to make sure to study if I'm not totally comfortable with the unit. I did enjoy good results with the algebra and problem solving units. I feel very happy and comfortable with algebra and I have no problems or reservations about doing algebra work. I think my ability to do math calculations has been consistent and has benefited from the work done this semester. Algebra and the related work was a good review of basic operations and integers. I have already discussed some specific work habits goals, like studying, correcting work, etc. I think I have had pretty good work habits all year. I always completed homework; I used class time effectively and finished a lot of work in class; I liked working in groups, but sometimes I have gotten off task. I think I need to stay focused in class, but it is hard because I can finish my work quickly and understand it. I need to let the people around me complete their work as well, so I don't deter them from it to talk instead. I think my current grade could be better, but it is probably an accurate mark for right now. I hope I do really well in this portfolio, because I put a lot of thought and effort into it. I also hope to do well on the final exam, which I will totally prepare myself for. I believe this portfolio is a very accurate reflection of myself and my abilities. I hope you enjoy looking through it and learn a little more about my math class and myself.

PLANNER F
STORING AND ORGANIZING PORTFOLIOS

Use this sheet to make and record decisions that fit the needs of your students and setting.

1. Where will your students store their portfolio entries?
   ☐ Pizza boxes
   ☐ Letter-size folders with pockets
   ☐ Legal-size file folders with stapled sides
   ☐ Plastic tote boxes with lids
   ☐ Folders made of heavy cardboard, stapled up the sides
   ☐ Laundry detergent boxes
   ☐ Cereal boxes
   ☐ Computer disks
   ☐ Hanging file folders
   ☐ Binders (with clear plastic pockets, pocket folders, or dividers)
   ☐ Accordion files
   ☐ Other _____

2. Where will the portfolios be stored?
   ☐ Shelves in your classroom
   ☐ Cupboards
   ☐ Filing cabinets
   ☐ Students' homes
   ☐ Other _____

3. What information will students include on the tracking form or working table of contents?
   ☐ Date
   ☐ Title of entry
   ☐ Intended audiences (teacher, peers, parents, family members)
   ☐ Categories
   ☐ Learning expectations
   ☐ Other _____

4. What type of introductory piece will be used?
   ☐ Graphic representation
   ☐ Fill-in-the blank
   ☐ Introductory letter
   ☐ Other _____

SHARING THE LEARNING

OVERVIEW

This chapter begins by providing a rationale for why students should share the learning evidenced in their portfolios. Ongoing communication of student learning serves a range of interested parties (especially those teachers, students, and parents who are directly involved) and often becomes the catalyst for joint celebration. Ways to share the portfolio with a variety of people are suggested, as well as informal and formal ways to respond to the learning. Sample instruments and forms are provided that are useful for structuring the sharing of specific entries as well as the entire portfolio. Sample written responses are also included to demonstrate how audiences can play a significant role in encouraging and extending learner thinking. **Planner G** helps you develop a plan for sharing.

WHY SHARE THE LEARNING?

The way into ideas, the way of making ideas truly one's own, is to be able to think them through, and the best way to do this is to talk them through. This talking is not merely a way of conveying existing ideas to others; it is also a way by which we explore ideas, clarify them, and make them our own.
—*M. Brubacher and R. Payne (1985)*

Sharing a portfolio is an ongoing conversation between the learner and a variety of key people in the learning process. It is not simply a one-time event that occurs at a parent-teacher conference. Portfolios should be shared over time with a variety of individuals including teachers, peers, parents, family members, and community leaders. The sharing process not only enables students to become more conscious about their learning and more precise in articulating it, the process also produces feedback from diverse perspectives. Such feedback, whether oral or written, assists students in reflecting on their competencies and skills, appreciating their growth and achievement, and setting future learning goals.

Options for ways to engage in portfolio conversations are numerous. Sharing, for instance, can focus on specific entries or on the entire portfolio,

PLANNER G
DARE TO SHARE

Use this form to record the decisions you've made while reading this chapter and to extend your thinking.

1. Identify the important partners who can participate in the portfolio sharing process. Use the following list to help you identify partners and indicate whether those partners will be involved in the process early (E) or late (L).

> The classroom teacher
> Peers within the class
> Peers from other classes
> Parents or relatives (e.g., grandparents or siblings)
> Important adults (e.g., family friends, neighbors, or youth group leaders)
> Educators in the school (e.g., administrators, counselors, or faculty)
> Educators in the district (e.g., central administrators or supervisors)
> Interested parties (e.g., community or business leaders, university professionals)

> _____

> _____

2. How will students begin to share selected entries? With whom will they share those items? Use the table below to map your plan. Start with simple procedures that will ensure early success. Work toward more elaborate procedures that will help your students develop sophisticated skills and challenge student thinking.

Sharing Individual Entries

Time Line	Sharing Procedures	The Audience	Response Procedures
In the beginning			
Steps in the middle			
Advanced stages			

THE PORTFOLIO ORGANIZER

3. How will the entire portfolio be shared? With whom will students share their portfolios? Use the table below to map your plan. Will the sharing be formal (e.g., a student-led conference with parents) or informal (e.g., a presentation or discussion in cooperative groups)? Consider the importance of your students having some practice before sharing. Again, start with simple sharing procedures that promote success, and build toward more elaborate procedures that will increase student thinking and learning.

Sharing the Entire Portfolio

Target Dates	Sharing Procedures	Practice Needed?	The Audience	Response Procedures
		☐ Yes ☐ No		
		☐ Yes ☐ No		
		☐ Yes ☐ No		

• What practical tips for sharing the learning have you gleaned from experienced portfolio users? Which of those tips will you try?

and it can be an informal conversation or a more formal written communication. The key is for sharing to occur regularly and for learners to have opportunities for both celebrating successes and identifying areas for growth. Sharing the learning with diverse audiences also allows the assessment process to become a public, shared, and cooperative endeavor. If a portfolio is a portrait of a learner, the involvement of others enriches that portrait because of the connections and discussions contributing to it. The broader the community for sharing, the richer the resource base for learners. Regardless of who is involved or how it takes place, sharing the learning ultimately results in deeper thinking and a clearer awareness of learning processes, performances, and needs.

PREPARING TO SHARE THE LEARNING

Whether sharing the entire portfolio or specific entries, the sharing process involves issues of trust, risk taking, and vulnerability. Help your students develop the interpersonal skills necessary to create conditions for trust and risk taking by preparing them to participate in the sharing and responding process. Preparation helps to ensure that the process will be positive, meaningful, and productive. The preparation for sharing that takes place in formal, structured conferences with teachers, parents, and other audiences is important and promotes successful informal, daily sharing in classrooms among peers. Practice, coaching, feedback, and processing prior to informal and formal sharing episodes contribute to the development of skills needed for the effective exchange of ideas. The following ideas illustrate ways to prepare participants to benefit from sharing.

INFORMAL SHARING

Model informal sharing. You may want to share an appropriate entry from your professional portfolio with your students. As the audience, your students can practice responding to what you have shared using positive sentence starters. Preparing your students for appropriate participation may include giving them sample sentence starters, such as those provided in **Figure 7.1**. To emphasize the importance of the students' responses to your portfolio and each other, you can express the feelings experienced, insights gained, or goals established during the sharing and responding.

Provide a warm-up activity prior to sharing. For example, have student partners generate a list of things they have in common, such as similar favorite collectibles, hobbies, or activities.

Facilitate cooperative interviews. Before sharing portfolio entries, have your students engage in cooperative three-step interviews (rotating the roles of interviewer, responder, and recorder) on one of the following topics: (1) What has someone you trust done to earn that trust? (2) Think back to special celebrations in your early childhood. Which celebration still makes you smile when you remember it? What made it so special? (3) What has been the proudest or happiest moment in your life? What led up to that moment?

Provide prompts and cues for sharing. Give your students time to review their work and select one item that they are particularly proud of (or liked, for whatever reason). Give students sample sentences starters to help them think about what they should say when they share their entries, such as

- I am proud of this work because . . .
- I want to share this item with you because . . .
- I feel good about this because . . .

Provide effective and ineffective sample peer responses. Discuss with students how each type of response would make them feel. Ask students to identify the responses that make them want to share and those responses that make them want to stop sharing. Ask them to discuss why they feel the way they do.

Provide prompts and cues for responding. Provide a sheet of positive sentence starters that students can use to respond to each other's work and give them copies of sample responses from peers (see **Figure 7.1**; **Appendix E** is a blank template).

FORMAL SHARING

Model the formal process that students will use to share. You may give a live demonstration or have students view a videotaped demonstration of portfolio conference. Highlight critical components of the process (e.g., create a list of steps) and teach the interpersonal skills needed for success (e.g., eye contact, listening). One way of modeling the formal process is to have a colleague come into the class and the two of you model the sharing of a portfolio entry.

Facilitate, videotape, and analyze practice conferences. Give students feedback on their conference performances and involve them in setting goals for improvement and refinement. For example, this can be done by providing two "wows" (strengths) and one "woe" (item to improve) after practice conferences.

Have students role-play formal sharing with learning buddies or peer tutors. Practice important skills such as greeting parents or other family members, managing time, and inviting responses from the audiences.

As a class, generate questions or a sample outline to be used by the audiences. The questions should promote positive dialogue between a learner and an audience that will lead to greater insights for everyone. Review the questions with your students prior to the conference and have them anticipate how they will address each question. For example, a sample outline could include questions such as "Can you tell me the easiest and most difficult aspects of maintaining your portfolio?" or "Can you share some of your most significant portfolio entries with me?"

Involve your students in the process of brainstorming possible questions that their audiences might ask. A wide variety of cooperative learning group strategies may be used to facilitate this brainstorming. In small groups, for example, each person can record a key question on an index card (each person may have multiple cards). The group can then review all questions and select the ones they most want to practice with prospective audiences. You might also have your students order the questions in a way that will promote success for them (e.g., simple to complex questions).

Have students prepare a sample interview agenda for a student-led conference (see **Appendix F**). Have students practice each step on the agenda with a partner, thereby providing each other with constructive feedback and suggestions for refinement.

Review and teach social skills that will contribute to the effectiveness of formal sharing. It is important for students to be aware of and to practice verbal and nonverbal skills. These skills include listening, encouraging, checking for understanding and other important interpersonal skills.

Develop and provide students with criteria for selecting entries to be shared in a formal conference. Such criteria need to be established early in the process. Ideally, students may work with the teacher to generate these criteria.

Set goals for the actual conference based on practice sessions. Helping students develop specific goals for a student-led conference is a challenging and important task. Goals may include giving an appropriate greeting to the audiences, following an agenda, clearly articulating reasons for entries, and inviting responses. (Chapter 8 provides additional ideas.)

FIGURE 7.1

Guiding Peer Response to Portfolio Entries

Use the sample starters to guide your students in responding to peers' portfolio entries.
Two student responses to peers' portfolio entries are given as examples.

Sample Starters

- I like . . .
- You have shown that you understand . . .
- Something that captured my attention . . .
- I want to know more about . . .
- Key words for me were . . .
- I particularly valued . . .
- A question raised in my mind is . . .(be positive in your inquiry)
- An idea that sparkled for me was . . .
- Something I identify with is . . .
- What I found especially meaningful was . . .
- Something you wrote that pushed my own thinking was . . .
- I learned that you . . . (something positive)
- Thank you for reminding me how important it is to . . .

When you write a response to a portfolio entry, please remember to give important details, such as your name and date of sharing. In addition, identify the entry to which you are responding (use the name or title of entry, or the date the sample entry was done by peer).

Sample Responses from Peers

Spelling, grammar, and punctuation have been preserved in the following peer responses to portfolio entries.

You have shown that you understand the concept of Scientific Notations and its uses. You also show that you are motivated by learning new material. IMPRESSIVE! While others might think that learning Scientific Notation is a waste of time, you on the other hand, understand that it is not garbage and that it will be useful sometime in the future. This entry was very well thought out and very detailed.

—*Ryoma, 10th grade Math class*

This is a great idea for an entry because it was a big group effort. As a member of your group for this project I can tell you that you did contribute a lot. This was a very productive project. You, Sharmila, will probably agree that our success in this project was because our other group members, more particularly Mike, stepped aside with his strong visual-spatial skills and let us participate.

—*Jessica, 7th grade Social Studies class*

SHARING INDIVIDUAL ENTRIES

Sharing individual entries with others, including the teacher, peers, parents, or other interested individuals, involves selecting which entries to share and explaining how those entries demonstrate growth or achievement. The reflections that students have prepared and attached to each learning sample (see Chapter 5) help students to think about what they have learned, whether criteria have been met, and what will be discussed during either informal or formal sharing opportunities. Sample sentence starters such as those below can be used to promote successful student sharing in beginning stages. For example, students can use sentence starters to prepare for and conduct oral interviews.

- This entry is . . .
- This entry is about . . .
- I created this item because . . .
- I chose this entry because . . .
- This is my most important or significant entry because . . .
- I want to share this entry with you because . . .

- This entry shows that I have accomplished . . .
- The most important thing I learned from this entry is . . .
- I am proud of this piece of work because . . .
- This entry shows that I know how to . . .
- This entry shows that I have improved in . . .
- This is the entry that best demonstrates use of . . . (a concept, skill, or principle)
- This entry shows that I have accomplished . . .
- This particular entry is meaningful to me because . . .
- In this entry, I want you to notice . . .
- This entry shows "before and after." I grew and progressed by . . .

RESPONDING TO ENTRIES

Any interested partners in the learning process can respond to specific entries that your students choose to share. For example, a peer might provide an oral affirmation regarding one aspect of a particular entry, or you might give helpful written suggestions for possible next steps on a project. Most teachers have been trained to respond to students' work in ways that highlight accomplishments and provide direction for improvement. Peers, parents, and other family members, however, may require support and assistance in this process. Providing structure for responses increases the likelihood that any audience will respond in ways that will be useful and meaningful for your students.

When beginning peer responses with your students, ask them to start with supportive and affirmative responses to promote the trust-building and self-disclosure that are essential to effective sharing. For learners to take risks and share both their successes and challenges with others, they need to feel that others respect them and value their efforts. The following suggestions for facilitating peer responses have been used successfully at various grade levels in the initial stages of sharing individual portfolio entries. For younger children, we suggest limiting the list of choices (e.g., provide three sentence starters) and asking students to select one to use for responding.

- A thought I especially liked is . . .
- I want to know more about . . .
- An idea that captured my interest is . . .
- Your entry shows . . . (something positive!)

For more ideas, see **Appendix E**.

TIPS FOR RESPONDING TO STUDENTS' WORK

Teachers and parents may benefit from receiving tips for providing effective feedback. The following list includes general suggestions for feedback, as well as specific sample starters for responding to students' work.

- Feedback should generate positive energy and motivation for continued learning.
- Ask students what they think, what helped them, and how they dealt with challenges.
- Focus on positive elements: What students value, sources of pride, and the criteria achieved.
- Use phrases that place students in a teaching role, such as "Help me to understand . . ." or "Show me . . ." or "Teach me what to do . . ." Such phrases foster elaboration, deeper reflection, and continued learning.
- Preface suggestions for improvement with phrases such as "I think that . . ." or "Try to . . ." to convey respect for student opinions and let students know that they own the problem and have choices about how to make improvements. For example, "I think that you need to try to write down more notes during the lesson" is better than "You are not taking enough notes during class."
- Try to make specific suggestions for improvement. For example, "Your answer to the equation needs to be reduced to lowest terms" is better than "You are not finished yet."
- End with a positive comment.

FIGURE 7.2

Feedback Starters

Use the following feedback starters to help you create the right atmosphere and
convey clear ideas about the portfolio to the student.

When You Agree with the Student
- Good point!
- That's a clear example of . . .
- I agree. It makes sense.
- That's the same reason I had in mind!
- I see how I can use that, too.

When You Disagree with the Student
- Here's another way of looking at the problem.
- I think there are some other things to consider.
- Yes, that's true; but it's not the only way.
- In addition, it's important to focus on . . .
- I'm not sure I agree; let's raise some questions together.

**When You Need to Encourage
a Discouraged Student**
- Keep going! You can do it!
- Let's talk it through together.
- Watch while I demonstrate.
- You give it a try and I'll help.

**When You Want to Convey Understanding
of the Student's Feelings**
- It makes you feel bad.
- It's so frustrating!
- It sounds as though you like . . .
- You're proud of your accomplishment!

When You Need to Suggest a Specific Change
- I'm not sure what you mean by this; try to think of an example that will help me understand.
- More information will help you make decisions; add . . .
- Proofread this part again; your partner can help you edit.
- This needs to be corrected; you have . . . instead of . . .
- Check that you have completed all parts.

adapted from B. Bower, *Portfolio Assessment and Evaluation*, 1994

Review **Figure 7.2** to help frame responses to students' portfolios. You can use these sentence starters and create your own to respond to students' portfolios with positive comments that encourage them and stretch their understanding and learning.

SAMPLE STARTERS FOR STRETCHING LEARNERS' THINKING

As your students become more experienced in responding to each other, their responses to entries should move beyond affirmation and encouragement to include questions or ideas that will stretch their peers' thinking. Unless you explicitly devote class time to helping students develop their questioning skills, however, you'll find it is difficult to deepen and extend the thinking of both the learners and the respondents. The following list provides sample prompts aimed at eliciting sophisticated and meaningful student responses. These prompts serve as models that are learned over time.

- Why is this particular accomplishment meaningful to you?

• How did you feel at the start? In the middle? When you finished?

• How has your accomplishment changed your thinking? Your life?

• What did you gain most from your experience?

• Walk me through your decision-making process.

• Where will this lead next?

• Compare and contrast your perspective with the one presented.

• Here is some new information; how does it connect with your information?

• Here is another example; how does it fit with what you explained?

• Predict what will happen if . . .

• Here's another idea to ponder . . . What do you think? What else can be added?

• Where else will this be useful?

WAYS TO SHARE AND RESPOND TO THE ENTIRE PORTFOLIO

How your students share their portfolios with others will depend on a range of factors, including the amount of time available, the number of students in your class (or classes), the expertise of you and your students in maintaining portfolios, and the capacity of other interested audiences to be involved in conferences or provide written feedback. Suggestions for ways students can share their entire portfolio with a variety of participants are listed below.

SHARING WITH THE TEACHER

• The student highlights key entries in a two-way conference with the teacher. After the conference, the teacher keeps the portfolio for further independent review and evaluation.

• The student and teacher have a two-way conference, during which time the teacher records

anecdotal comments for the purposes of evaluation (e.g., report cards and parent feedback).

• The teacher responds to the entire portfolio in a written response.

• The teacher responds to the entire portfolio by completing an evaluation rubric (created and shared with students at the beginning of the process—see Chapter 9).

• The teacher interviews four students simultaneously. During the interviews, the students observe and record pertinent information (see **Appendix G**). At the end of the interview session, each student receives oral feedback from the teacher and the other students. Students may also give each other copies of the comments they recorded during the interviews.

SHARING WITH PEERS

• Pairs share portfolios and provide written feedback to each other, possibly using a form provided by the teacher.

• Pairs share portfolios and provide oral feedback to each other, possibly based on a rubric developed by the teacher and the class.

• A triad of students interview each other (the roles of interviewer, sharer, and recorder rotate). At the end of all three interviews, each student receives oral feedback from group members. Written peer comments are also given to each student. Peers are encouraged to congratulate each other and celebrate their learning.

See **Appendix H** for helpful tips for sharing portfolios with peers.

SHARING WITH PARENTS OR SIGNIFICANT ADULTS

• The portfolio is sent home with a brief letter that explains the process. In this letter, an adult is asked to evaluate the portfolio using a structured form provided by the teacher.

• Parents are invited to the school for a student-led conference that uses the portfolio as evidence of learning. In this conference, parents are encouraged to acknowledge and affirm their child's learning. The teacher can guide the verbal conversation and follow up with a written record of key points discussed.

- Parents are invited to the school for a student-involved conference where the teacher orchestrates the conference and the student is involved in various ways (e.g., having certain portfolio items ready to share, or articulating a goal.)

- Parents are invited to an Evening of Celebration, which involves parents congregating in one large area where students enter in a procession carrying gift-wrapped portfolios. Students present the portfolios to their parents as "a gift of my effort and achievement."

See **Appendix I** for helpful tips for sharing portfolios with parents or significant adults.

SHARING WITH OTHER AUDIENCES

- Students can share their learning with peers across classes. Buddy systems among classes are arranged so that students can share their learning with their buddies. Cross-class meetings occur regularly to promote the development of ongoing, supportive relationships for sharing.

- School administrators set aside a regular period of time and invite individuals or groups of students to share their portfolios.

One of the most powerful ways for students to share their portfolios with others is through student-led conferences. Use **Activity 9** to help you think through the key components of effective student-led conferences. **Figure 7.3** contains ideas that were generated in a discussion between two middle school teachers who have experimented with student-led conferencing.

There are other ways to share the learning with other students and adults in your community. Review the following figures to see if the ideas fit your needs. Use **Planner G** (pp. 60–61) to think about audiences as you make plans to share the learning and use various opportunities to include parents and other people in the portfolio process (**figures 7.4, 7.5,** and **7.6**). **Figure 7.7** offers students guidance in reflecting upon the student–teacher–parent conference. **Appendix J** offers a simple, guided feedback form for the student, peer, parent, and teacher.

As with all your first steps in planning portfolio assessment, the forms, checklists, and samples provided in this chapter are to help you, your students, and other audiences prepare for sharing the learning. When students first begin to share either specific entries or their entire portfolios with audiences, the structured forms provide guidance for audience members to help ensure that a positive interactive process of learning occurs. The forms also increase the chances that students will be guided in successful directions.

ACTIVITY 9
Generating the Components of a Student-Led Conference

This activity provides an opportunity for you and your colleagues to identify the important components of effective student-led conferences. You'll need paper for recording notes and you may choose to view a videoclip of a student-led conference (e.g., from *Redesigning Assessment Series* [ASCD, 1992]). If you choose that optional activity, you'll need a VCR and television. (We suggest 9 or more participants.) See **Figure 7.3** for a sample response to this activity.

1. Gather into groups of three teachers who teach the same grade level and assign each person a number from one to three. A facilitator may ease the transition from large to small groups.

2. Option 1. In small groups, brainstorm ideas about elements important to a successful student-led conference based on your combined knowledge or experiences.

Option 2. View a short videoclip of a student-led conference. As you view the video, jot down what you think are the key elements or steps of the conference (e.g., students introducing their parents to the teacher). At the end of the videoclip, combine your ideas with those of your group on the team recording sheet. If possible, add other ideas that are important to you.

3. Reach consensus on about six components that would be most significant for your students. Ensure that each group member can articulate the rationale for each item on your list. One person will be randomly selected to share the list and rationale with another group.

4. The facilitator chooses a number from one to three and asks the person with that number from each group to stand. When the facilitator calls "Point and Switch," each standing "ambassador" points to another group's ambassador. When two ambassadors are pointing to each other, they have agreed to exchange groups. Each ambassador joins a new group and shares the previous team's consensus and rationales with that group. Everyone discusses the differences and similarities of their lists.

5. The facilitator debriefs with the large group and leads a discussion about how teachers can introduce, practice, and refine the selected component parts in preparation for successful student-led conferencing.

FIGURE 7.3

Sample Response to Activity 9 (Components of a Student-Led Conference)

The following ideas are from a discussion between two middle school teachers who have experimented with student-led conferences. The ideas were generated while doing the exercise in **Activity 9**.

Identifying Components of the Student-Led Conference

- Welcome areas where parents and students can wait comfortably
- Physical environment for interview is comfortable and familiar (especially for students)
- Introduction of parents and teacher by student
- Agenda for interview prepared by student
- Agenda includes discussion of student's strengths and weaknesses, as well as time for parent concerns, adequate time for student to present portfolio, and time for teacher comments
- A "prepared way" to bring the interview to a close
- Student is prepared for possible questions parents might ask and is able to answer them
- Student is prepared to help parents generate questions if they aren't sure what to ask
- Teacher has a supportive strategy to help a struggling student
- Opportunity for follow-up meetings with parents who need or request more time or a private interview

Essential Components of a Conference

After brainstorming the above list, my partner and I agreed on the following essential components for an effective student-led conference:

- Student introduces parents and teacher to each other
- Student has prepared agenda that allows time to discuss strengths, areas of growth and challenges, parent concerns, and teacher comments
- A prepared, effective, courteous way to bring the interview to a close
- A subtle, supportive, and effective strategy for the teacher to help the student who struggles in the conference (e.g., the teacher asks questions that will help direct the student to important points in the agenda)
- Student has anticipated questions a parent might ask and is prepared to answer them

Figure 7.4

Home Portfolio Review

Use a variation of the following letter to ask an adult, who is significant in the student's life, to review the student's portfolio. A structured form makes the response easier for the adult and provides positive feedback needed by the student. This sample illustrates a parent's response to her daughter's learning in mathematics.

Letter of Explanation

Dear Reader:

All students taking Grade 9 Mathematics at our school have compiled portfolios of work. Each student's portfolio should include at least 10 pieces of best work. Please note that the students have had the opportunity to correct errors and to catch up on missing work before submitting the portfolio for final evaluation. The portfolio is worth 10 percent of the final grade in the course.

The Mathematics portfolios are evaluated by the teacher, the student, and by one other person (you). Thank you for taking the time to read this portfolio and to evaluate it. The students and I use a scoring rubric for evaluation purposes, but we ask you to complete the enclosed form. Please include brief comments as well as scores in all of the categories. Please send your evaluation to me by April 20.

Thank you very much for your participation. Please call me at 800-0000 if you have any questions or concerns.

Sincerely,

A. Teacher
Mathematics Department

FIGURE 7.4 (continued)

Sample Portfolio Review Form

Name of student: <u>Christine Gusterson</u>

Name of evaluator: <u>Lu-Anne Gusterson</u>

Date: <u>April 15</u>

Relationship to student: <u>Mother</u>

Please indicate your evaluation by circling the appropriate number on each scale. Space has been provided for comments about the student's work. Thank you for taking the time to provide the student with valuable feedback.

1. Neatness and Organization of Work

10	⑨		8	7		6	5		4	3	2	1
Superior			Proficient			Adequate			Limited			

Reasons:
I found your portfolio to be extremely neat and well organized. I liked the chronological order used as I saw for myself how you were progressing through the subjects covered.

2. Quality of Work

10	⑨		8	7		6	5		4	3	2	1
Superior			Proficient			Adequate			Limited			

Reasons:
Excellent work habits were demonstrated throughout your portfolio. Pen, pencil, color pencils, and ruling were used properly. Corrections and proofing were done in a neat and orderly fashion. Original work was very well done.

3. Evidence of Effort

10	⑨		8	7		6	5		4	3	2	1
Superior			Proficient			Adequate			Limited			

Reasons:
Your efforts are shown all the way through your portfolio by the neatness, organization, and your comments on your reflection sheets. Your honesty is great!

4. Please indicate which item in the portfolio impressed you the most and give reasons for your choice.

I cannot pick one item . . . you see, if you were not my daughter, I would have felt like your best friend reading your diary (with your permission, of course). Your honesty, joys, disappointments, frustration, and excitement are clearly evident throughout your portfolio. Your efforts, organization, neatness, and style lend the reader to a better understanding and a mental picture of you trying to grasp, learn, understand, develop, and communicate new skills in math as well as other subjects on a daily basis. Keep up the good work and good luck on your exam.

TOTAL: 27 / 30

FIGURE 7.5

Adult Portfolio Review and Response

At the end of a student-involved conference, ask the parent or adult to acknowledge and affirm the student's learning based on evidence in the portfolio. The first sample response is a translation of a non-English speaking parent's response to her son's work. Spelling, grammar, and punctuation have been preserved.

Name of Reviewer: _____   Date: _____

1. Please record two successes or sources of pride as you review the student's portfolio.

   Dear Haseeb:
   I am very happy with your progress. I am really grateful to your teacher, who with her hard work and dedication, has put you to a point, where by the grace of God, you'd be starting your grade one. I pray that you succeed like this throughout your life.

2. Please record one wish for your child's growth.

   You take special care in your studies, always strive for the best, and study with your heart. May God guide you and make you successful.

   —Haseeb's mother

Template adapted from Davies, Cameron, Politano, and Gregory, 1992.

FIGURE 7.6

Parent and Student Review

The following is an example of how two parents responded to their daughter's portfolio. This response became a valued item in the student's portfolio and contributed to the subsequent student reflection on the entire conference experience **(Figure 7.7)**.

Please take the time to have your child present the portfolio to you. Ask questions about it: What makes your child proud of it? What has been a challenge? Then complete this form and discuss it with your child. Please remember to keep your comments positive and constructive because this should be a celebration of your child's accomplishments.

If English is not your first language, you may choose to complete this form in your native language. Perhaps your child or a friend can give a brief translation on the back of the form.

1. As you review your child's portfolio, what makes you particularly proud of your child?

The effort Lina has displayed and put forth in her math work has made us very proud. Also, the Tide and Sunlight Project which Lina did allowed us to see how well she was able to organize an experiment and perform it.

2. What is the most important change you have seen in your child this year?

The most important change that we have noted is that Lina has been able to adapt very well to this new school year. We realize that this year is much more demanding than last year, and we are glad Lina has been able to make such a good adjustment.

FIGURE 7.7

Student Reflection Sheet

After having a conference with the teacher and parent, the student is expected to take some time to reflect upon this learning experience by answering the following questions in detail. The following example preserves the student's spelling, grammar, and punctuation.

Name of Student: __Lina__   **Date of Conference:** <u>**Thursday, Dec. 3, 8 p.m.**</u>

1. How did you prepare for this conference?

I prepared for this conference by using a planning sheet and saying what I wanted to do in the 20 minutes that I had. I also prepared for the conference by practicing with my two friends as though one was my mom and other one was the teacher but really an observer to tell me things I can improve in.

2. Do you think you were adequately prepared for the conference?

Yes, I do think I was adequately prepared for this conference because I practiced many times at school with my friends. Also with the things the observer saw I improved in them so I wouldn't do them in the interview. I also had the planning sheet to help me through the conference so I do think I was adequately prepared.

3. What changes would you make for your next conference?

Some changes I would make in my next conference would be to talk about some other things because I had a lot of extra time. I would also talk about my weakness and strength and something I'm improving in more because I just said what they were and didn't talk about them very much.

4. What did you learn about yourself as a learner in this conference?

Something I learned about myself in this conference was that I keep almost the whole class on task well that's what the teacher said. The only thing is I can't keep myself on task.

5. During the conference, were there any learning goals established? If yes, state them. If no, can you develop any goals as a result of the conference?

Yes, there were some learning goals established in the conference. One of the goals was to read from a variety of books, not just one kind. Another goal is to participate more in small and big class discussions.

SETTING GOALS

8

KEY IDEAS

- Identifying the importance of goal setting
- Exploring elements of effective goal setting
- Sample goal-setting forms

OVERVIEW

This chapter is designed to help you examine the importance of goal setting in the overall portfolio process. You'll learn about a theoretical model that places goal setting in the context of effective self-evaluation and the eight key elements that help you support students in the process of goal setting. Within the chapter, the activities and examples help you learn techniques that facilitate goal setting in a variety of classroom settings. Use the forms to help you consolidate decisions and extend your thinking related to the goal-setting component of portfolio use.

WHY STUDENTS NEED GOALS

According to work in the 1970s by Bernard Weiner and colleagues, achievement motivation "is based on the proposition that the way persons come to *perceive* and to *interpret* the causes of their successes or failures are the major determinants of

their achievement motivation, rather than fixed early experiences" (Arends, 1991, p. 109). Weiner suggests that success or failure can be attributed to four causes: ability, effort, luck, and the difficulty of the learning task. One of the main messages that can be taken from his work is the difference between internal and external locus of control. Students who attribute success to variables within their control exert more effort. These students, for example, attribute their success to their abilities and their failure to a lack of effort. Students who have high achievement seem to believe they have control (internal control) over their achievement. Other students, however, often believe that success is connected to luck and that failure is attributed to lack of ability that they can't overcome through their own efforts. Students with low achievement motivation seem to fall in the second category and believe success is related to external controls (Arends, 1991).

Weiner's theory supports the idea that you can take steps in the classroom to increase a child's motivation to learn. You can carry out practices in the classroom that may change students' perceptions of themselves and thereby increase the effort they put into learning. One way to increase motivation is to introduce self-evaluation, which gives students greater control over their work. For example, when students are provided with opportunities to self-evaluate their work as part of the portfolio process (e.g., reflecting on work, judging

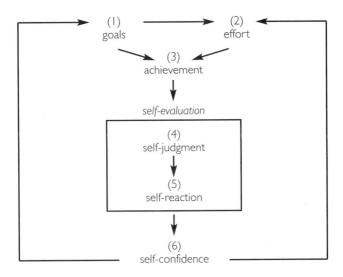

FIGURE 8.1

How Self-Evaluation Contributes to Learning

When students evaluate their performance positively, those self-evaluations encourage students to set higher goals (1) and to commit more personal resources or effort (2) to them. The combination of goals (1) and effort (2) equals achievement (3). A student's achievement results in self-judgment (4), such as a student contemplating the question, "Were my goals met?" The result of the self-judgment is self-reaction (5), or a student responding to the judgment with the question, "How do I feel about that?" Goals, effort, achievement, self-judgment, and self-reaction combine to affect self-confidence (6) in a positive way.

(adapted from Rolheiser, 1996, p. 4)

achievement toward identified criteria, and establishing goals), they become engaged in a process that can powerfully affect their motivation. Why? Because a positive self-evaluation encourages students to set higher goals and make a strong commitment to reaching them, as shown in **Figure 8.1**.

Studies indicate that when students have been taught how to self-evaluate and set goals, their achievement (e.g., improvement in narrative writing) is significantly higher than that of students who have not been taught to self-evaluate and set

goals (Ross, Rolheiser, & Hogaboam-Gray, 2000). Providing opportunities for students to set goals can support an upward cycle of learning as indicated in **Figure 8.1.** Setting goals helps students who have negative orientations toward learning or who do not have realistic views of their strengths and weaknesses. Teachers can help these students by establishing appropriate goals, selecting effective learning strategies to reach those goals, committing effort toward those goals, and celebrating the results of their performances. Lyra, a 10th grade student, articulates the value of goal setting:

I found the goal setting sheets help me a lot in understanding and recognizing my math skills. Setting goals for yourself helps you identify your strengths and weaknesses and makes you aware of them. Having personal goals also gives you a strong sense of your capabilities and helps you motivate yourself to make the most out of them. For me, it made me realize that you do have to work to accomplish your goals, but in the end it is worth it.

Rolheiser (1996) identifies a four-stage model for teaching students better self-evaluation skills. The fourth stage of the model involves assisting students as they develop goals and accompanying action plans based on their self-evaluations.

The most difficult part of teaching students how to evaluate their work consists of designing ways to provide support for students as they use self-evaluative data to set new goals and levels of effort. Without teacher help, students may be uncertain whether they have attained their goals. Teachers can also help students to connect particular levels of achievement to the learning strategies they have adopted and to the effort they have expended. Finally, teachers can help students to develop viable action plans in which feasible goals are operationalized as a set of specific action intentions. The specific steps to guide this stage are as follows:

1. students identify strengths and weaknesses
2. students generate goals
3. teacher guides students to develop specific actions towards their goals
4. students' goals and action plans are recorded

(Rolheiser, 1996, p. 6)

Figure 8.2 is an example of a goal-setting form that may be easily adapted for a variety of settings. A blank template of this goal-setting sheet is included as **Appendix K.**

STEPS TO EFFECTIVE GOAL SETTING

Given how challenging most students and teachers find the process of goal setting, it is essential to consider eight key elements: timeliness, specificity, attainability, record keeping, reflection, long-term and short-term goals, feeling tone, and modeling effective goal setting.

1. Timeliness. As you use portfolios with students, you'll need to review key assessment and evaluation dates, such as report card distributions, parent-teacher conferences, and community curriculum evenings. Key dates influence the planning of appropriate time lines for goal setting.

Allow some time at the beginning of a course or year of study before students are expected to set appropriate goals for learning. Delaying the process allows students time to be engaged in enough learning experiences to compile processes, products, and feedback from others. In addition, if goal setting is new to students, you need time to introduce it and to model how it is going to be carried out. This initial time period also allows you to become familiar with students' strengths and weaknesses so that you can assist the students in choosing effective goals. As with many of the assessment approaches teachers use, decisions need to be made regarding the frequency and manageability of goal setting.

2. Specificity. The most frequent problem teachers express about student goal setting is that the goals are too broad and cannot be measured easily. For example, students often set the goal of "working harder." This goal is not only too vague, it is also extremely difficult to measure, which makes it nearly impossible to determine if students have reached that particular goal. For students new to goal setting, teacher modeling is invaluable. Your role may be to brainstorm with the whole class what a goal looks like in action. For the example given, this might include saying to

FIGURE 8.2

Sample of a Student's Goal Setting Sheet

See **Appendix K** for a blank template.

Name: Kim   Date: September 30

Area of Focus: 10th grade Mathematics

Strengths:
• Reviewing notes before class
• I work well on my own . . . I concentrate!
• I try to learn from my mistakes

Challenges:
• I don't always ask for help
• Paying attention to proper form
• I give up when I'm frustrated
• Keeping up with work

My Goal:
• To improve my work habits

What will I do to achieve my goal?
• Study for tests instead of just quickly looking over my notes
• Do practice questions while I'm studying
• Try to figure stuff out myself first, but then get extra help from my teacher or friends.

Target date: November 30

(template adapted from Rolheiser, 1996, p. 94)

the class, "What would I actually see you doing if you were working harder? Generate as many actions as you can." Students might come up with the ideas of completing homework regularly and recording that action on a log, staying on task during group work, or completing and correcting a review before a test. Students can then select one or two specific actions that are the most productive for them.

3. Attainability. One of the factors that can influence a student's achievement motivation is the feeling of success. Success is associated with both the degree of difficulty of the task and the amount of effort given (Arends, 1991). If students feel that a goal is too easy and requires too little effort, they may not feel motivated or experience feelings of success. Conversely, if goals are too broad or too difficult for students, students may not feel motivated or have success. Vague or inappropriate goals may be challenging to measure and may also create a great deal of frustration.

Your role with students is to help them select goals that are realistic, achievable, and challenging. Meeting with students about their goals is a crucial activity in this process. During these meetings, use your active listening skills and engage in probing, clarifying, and other questioning skills to ensure that students' goals are focused and achievable. Students who set very high goals may need to be encouraged to rethink those goals (e.g., impossibly lofty goals can become a series of smaller goals). Similarly, if students always set low goals, work with them to set higher expectations.

4. Record keeping. Unrecorded goals are not particularly helpful. In the hectic pace of a classroom and with all that transpires in one day, oral comments may be forgotten or misinterpreted. When learners can refer back to recorded goals, they can more easily assess their progress and achievement.

5. Reflection. Revisiting goals gives learners opportunities to monitor and adjust their learning strategies and the goals. As individuals become proficient at developing appropriate goals, adjustments may not be necessary or as difficult. When learners have the chance to reflect by themselves and articulate their goals and action plans to other audiences, reflection is more powerful than when done alone.

6. Short-term and long-term goals. Students can generate both long-term and short- term goals. Short-term goals can be met in a limited time frame, such as before an upcoming portfolio conference. Short-term goals tend to be motivating because students believe they can achieve them in the foreseeable future. Again, success is a power-

ful motivator. Nevertheless, you also need to help students value working toward goals that are not immediately attainable. One benefit of using portfolios is that learners can see tangible evidence of setting goals and documenting their growth and achievement over time.

7. Feeling tone. "Feeling tones in the classroom are not only the result of specific things teachers say at a particular moment; they are also the result of many other structures and processes created by teachers to produce productive learning environments" (Arends, 1994, p. 117). Feeling tones are created by variables ranging from specific things you may say or do as a teacher to the daily actions demonstrated by peers. What is clear is that students put forth more or less effort toward goals depending on the tone of the learning environment. Portfolio assessment is most powerful when the structures and processes that are inherent in the process contribute to a productive learning environment. When students can engage in setting goals that do not lead to comparisons or win-lose relationships, but rather help establish cooperative goal structures and positive interdependence, then the result is an environment conducive to learning. Goal setting that is a shared classroom activity (e.g., it is public and has many interested, collaborating parties) encourages students to put more effort into goal setting and, accordingly, into achievement of those goals.

8. Modeling effective goal setting. For students who are new to goal setting, provide examples of different types of goals and give them the opportunity to discuss the attributes of those goals. An activity that engages students in comparing effective and less effective goal statements can help them to begin to discern the qualities inherent to successful goal setting. You can also videotape exemplary goal-setting conferences and have the students watch and think about what contributes to the determination of focused goals.

ACTIVITY 10
What's in a Goal?

Reflecting on a goal you've achieved can be useful in identifying actions and variables that helped you attain that goal. You can use that information to determine elements that might be key in attaining future goals. You may want to use a concept web to record your thoughts. **Figure 8.3** offers an example of a complete concept web that resulted from this activity.

1. Find a partner and work through the activity together. One partner interviews and records the responses of the other partner. If a concept web is used, record the accomplishment in the center, then record additional responses on various branches or subbranches. Ask probing questions to determine how the responses should be classified or connected to the web.

2. Interview: Name an accomplishment of which you are particularly proud (insert in center circle on the web).

What specific actions did you take to achieve this goal, or what variables con-

tributed to your accomplishment? (Record these answers as branches and subbranches on the concept web.)

3. When the concept web is complete, reverse roles and repeat the process.

4. With your partner, examine both concept webs and extract major considerations, key ideas, and common themes that helped you both accomplish your goals.

5. Discuss how these variables relate to the goal-setting process for students. Would this activity be helpful for your students to experience? Elaborate on your responses.

REFLECTING ON GOALS

Activity 10 contains an effective method for reflecting on a goal that you have achieved and the variables that contributed to that success. If you are working with a team, examine your collective experiences to determine the components of successful goal setting. You can adapt this activity for students by tapping into their successes in achieving goals and examining them for specific actions that contributed to the successes. Using this activity helps students examine concrete examples that will guide their future goal setting. Attributes of effective goal setting can be posted in your classroom and thus be available throughout the portfolio process.

In **Figure 8.3,** Carol interviews Barb about an accomplishment. Using a concept web, Carol records Barb's ideas. After the web is completed, the colleagues extract key ideas about what contributed to Barb's accomplishment.

Teachers can support the goal-setting process by providing structure for students. In addition to the techniques outlined in this chapter, you can

FIGURE 8.3

Sample Response to Activity 10 (What's in a Goal?)

A concept web is an effective way of examining a past success to determine the elements that might be key in attaining a future goal. Carol devised the following web when she interviewed Barb about having an article published in a journal. See **Activity 10** for instructions designed to help you produce your own web.

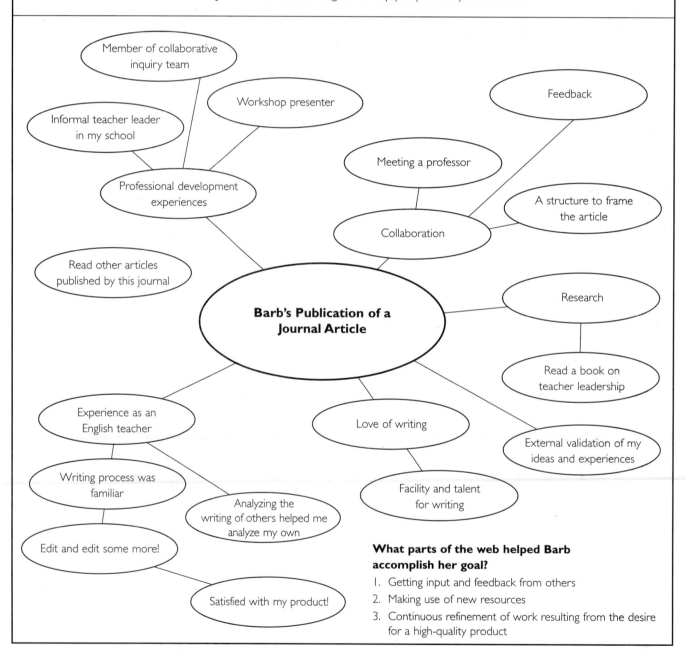

What parts of the web helped Barb accomplish her goal?

1. Getting input and feedback from others
2. Making use of new resources
3. Continuous refinement of work resulting from the desire for a high-quality product

use the forms in **Appendix L** to provide structure for your students. Adjust the ideas to fit the age and maturity levels of your students. Matt, a 10th grade student, articulates some attributes of goal setting:

> I feel the goal-setting sheet in the algebra portfolio helped a lot. It gave me something to strive for. I looked back on the goals sheet midway through the semester and realized one of my goals was already completed. By the end of the semester all my goals were achieved and I wouldn't have realized it, if it weren't for the goal-setting sheet.

Reflection can contribute to students' knowledge of themselves as learners. That knowledge, used in self-evaluation and goal setting, affects students' perceptions and interpretations of what causes their successes and failures. Self-perception and interpretation, in turn, affect achievement motivation. Practical steps in the classroom, such as those taken while working on a portfolio, can enhance students' motivation. Important steps include structuring support for students to set and achieve goals. Structured support may include providing worksheets that help guide students toward the goals, and engaging students in collaborative goal setting activities throughout portfolio assessment. **Planner H** presents a list of questions that can help you think through how you will set the stage for goal setting in your portfolio model.

PLANNER H
SETTING THE STAGE FOR GOALS

Use this list of questions to help you establish the groundwork for goals in your portfolio model.

1. What is your rationale for goal setting and how will you communicate this to your students?

2. When will goal setting begin?

3. How often will formal goal setting occur?

4. What specific methods will you use to model goal setting for students?

5. What techniques and forms will you use or adapt for your students?

EVALUATION AND GRADING

OVERVIEW

In this chapter, we present ideas to help you explore the values and beliefs inherent in evaluation and grading issues. Key questions and activities provide a framework to guide your decision making about the evaluation and grading of portfolios. As you review the criteria for evaluating portfolios (from Chapter 3), two scenarios illustrate ways to involve students in the evaluation process. You'll be introduced to the concept of evaluation rubrics and given suggestions for how to develop portfolio rubrics. We outline practical approaches to both evaluation and grading, and include sample forms to help you get started.

THE PHILOSOPHY OF ASSESSMENT, EVALUATION, AND GRADING

Three terms commonly used in professional discussions are assessment, evaluation, and grading. Unfortunately, there is not always a clear understanding of what each term means. The definitions in **Figure 9.1** clarify the use of these terms in this book. Teachers, students, and parents all can benefit from a shared understanding of these terms.

If assessment is defined as the gathering of data about students' learning, then a portfolio is a form of assessment. Because the portfolio is in part a method of collecting data, the portfolio process becomes a process of assessment. When making decisions about evaluating and grading portfolios, realize that your philosophy regarding general questions of evaluation and grading affects the approach you take with portfolios. Many variables affect your general philosophy, including what you believe to be the purpose of evaluation and grading, your experiences as a student, the practices used in the school environment, and public accountability policies and procedures. Your beliefs, attitudes, and practices combine to form your evaluation and grading philosophy. Your philosophy will not be static; in fact, it will be affected by your implementation of portfolio assessment.

Michael Fullan (Fullan & Stiegelbauer, 1991) identifies three components in implementing any

FIGURE 9.1

Definitions

Although the following terms are frequently used by educators, they are not always clearly defined.
Use these definitions to ensure common understanding and facilitate discussions with your colleagues.

Assessment: gathering data

Evaluation: judging merits

Grading: assigning values to symbols for reporting

new idea or policy: (1) the possible use of new or revised materials; (2) the possible use of new teaching approaches, strategies, or activities; and (3) the possible alteration of beliefs. What this means in your implementation of portfolio assessment is that, as you adopt new materials (e.g., reflection sheets or goal-setting instruments) and practices (e.g., collaborative assessment or inviting parents to respond to student work), your philosophy or beliefs can shift. As Fullan suggests, "all three aspects of change are necessary because together they represent the means of achieving a particular educational goal or set of goals" (Fullan & Stiegelbauer, 1991, p. 37). Achieving these goals can be challenging and complex, especially given the inevitable shifts in assessment, evaluation, grading, and your practices and beliefs. For teachers, the question of how to evaluate or grade portfolios is likely the most challenging issue related to the implementation of portfolios. **Activity 11** is designed to help you make key decisions related to assessment and evaluation issues. Revisit your decisions as you gain experience with portfolio assessment.

ACTIVITY 11
Beginning with Beliefs

Your beliefs greatly influence the approach you take to assessment, evaluation, and grading. Answer these questions to crystallize your thinking about your beliefs and actions related to assessment, evaluation, and grading.

1. What effect did grading have on you as a student in elementary school? Middle school? High school? College? How did grading make you feel?

_____

_____

_____

_____

2. What do you believe is the purpose of evaluation? Grading?

_____

_____

_____

_____

3. What evidence of student learning do you now collect?

_____

_____

_____

_____

4. Do you believe that students will not work unless the work is graded?

_____

_____

_____

_____

5. What concerns, issues, or questions do you have about evaluation or grading? What challenges and frustrations have you faced? What successes have you experienced?

_____

_____

_____

_____

6. How do you make decisions about what will be graded?

_____

_____

_____

_____

7. If you are a parent, what have you noticed about how your child reacts to evaluation and grading practices? How have you reacted as a parent?

_____

_____

_____

_____

8. Do you believe that teachers should do everything in their power to deemphasize grades? In what ways do you act on your beliefs?

_____

_____

_____

_____

9. What is the single most important goal for you as a teacher when evaluating or grading your students?

_____

_____

_____

_____

10. Make a note of other personal reflections related to grading and evaluation.

_____

_____

_____

_____

_____

_____

_____

_____

PARTICIPANTS IN THE EVALUATION OR GRADING PROCESS

Who is now involved in evaluation and grading decisions in your classroom? As you implement portfolio assessment, you'll want to consider the people who might participate in the process. Naturally, the most important partner is the student. You and your students need to be involved in the process from the beginning; other participants may include parents, peers in the same classroom, peers in other grades, significant adults, and school administrators.

If you view decision making about evaluation and grading as a series of steps, you see that the combination of participants can vary with each step. For example, in the first step, students may have a voice in the development of the criteria used to evaluate or judge their portfolios. You also play an important role in that criteria development. At a later step, when the portfolios are ready to be shared, peers and parents may play a role. The final step of grading (if grading occurs) may be your sole responsibility as you also consider peer evaluations and self-evaluations.

As you explore this chapter, identify potential partners in the portfolio process. As you become experienced with the process, you may expand the network of partners.

CRITERIA FOR EVALUATING PORTFOLIOS

There are two major ways to determine the criteria for evaluating the portfolios. Your experience with portfolios, your willingness to take risks, and your students' age and experience with portfolios, contribute to how criteria are chosen. Consider the following scenarios that illustrate these two approaches for determining criteria.

Scenario 1. Students do not have experience with developing portfolios, therefore they do not have a clear sense of what criteria might be relevant in the evaluation of those portfolios. Consequently, you need to take the lead in determining evaluation criteria. Consider the purpose, type, and categories of the portfolio, as well as the expectations or outcomes targeted for learning. See Chapter 3 for a list of generic criteria (e.g., knowledge of content, organization and presentation, self-assessment and goal setting, completeness). Use only a few criteria to ensure manageability for you and success for students.

After selecting relevant criteria early in the process, you'll need to explain them to students. They must have a clear understanding of the criteria. You may invite students to respond to an initial criteria list, and the ensuing class discussion can be useful in clarifying terminology and revising the list to incorporate student-friendly language.

Scenario 2. Students have experience with portfolios and can participate in choosing appropriate criteria. You can invite students to select a few criteria from a list, such as the one in Chapter 3. Or, you and your students can negotiate the criteria from a list you generate together (Rolheiser, 1996). For example, negotiation might begin when you choose one or two criteria important for the learning expectations or outcomes that you have targeted and the students generate additional criteria that are important to them. Another technique is for the students to prioritize criteria from the list. Following that step, you can choose the criteria and include at least a few of their highest priorities. Many variations of this process are possible; the key is for the final list to be a result of negotiation. For example, in a mathematics portfolio for 9th graders, a teacher can choose a problem-solving criterion because it is an important component in achieving the learning outcomes of the course. Students might choose additional criteria such as organization, completeness, and connections to science and technology.

PORTFOLIO RUBRICS

As educators shift their assessment and evaluation practices, rubrics are becoming popular. Many definitions abound for "rubrics," including "a scale that includes achievement criteria and descriptions of levels of quality; used to assess and evaluate students' work and guide students to desired achievement level" (Clemens, workshop notes, 1999). Another is "a series of narrative statements describing the levels of quality of a product or a performance" (Educators in Connecticut's Pomperaug Regional School District 15, 1996, p. 279). In general terms, a rubric is a guideline for determining how well students are performing particular tasks. "It is, most commonly, a scoring device which allows a judge (a teacher or other audience) to distinguish how effectively students are performing assigned tasks" (Johnson, 1996, p. 143).

The use of a rubric helps all parties (students, teachers, peers, and parents) because it clarifies criteria, expectations, and expected standards of quality for a performance or product. It also helps teachers with planning by focusing on instruction and connecting it to assessment. Rubrics help students think critically about their own learning and the learning of their peers by providing a framework for self-assessment and peer assessment. Rubrics specify and facilitate the evaluation and grading process. "The most critical step in the development of a scoring rubric for evaluating student performance is its initial design. For this process, a number of factors—such as whether it is generic or specific, the actual criteria, the number of points on the scale, and the language used to define the points—must be taken into account" (Danielson, 1997, p. 65). Rubrics can be used with learners of all ages, with adjustments made to reflect their ages and abilities. For example, language can be simplified, criteria limited, and graphics or icons used to represent ideas. The lay-out and spacing of the rubric may also affect the appropriateness for a particular age group. The following guidelines (Wiggins, workshop notes, 1993) are helpful for rubric construction.

GUIDELINES FOR RUBRIC CONSTRUCTION

A rubric is a *set of scoring guidelines* for evaluating student work. The rubric answers an important question: What does mastery (and varying degrees of mastery) of a task look like? While devising a rubric, it is important to consider the following points:

• The rubric must enable judges and performers to discriminate effectively between performances of different quality.

• The language at each level should clearly describe each level of performance; avoid comparative language (e.g., not as good as level 3) and evaluative language (e.g., excellent, good).

• The two most important points on the scale are the top point (describing genuine excellence) and the cut point (describing the difference between passing and failing).

• The descriptions of each point on the scale should represent a smooth continuum from the previous description to the next, as much as possible.

• The dilemma lies in choosing a generic or task-specific rubric. The more task-specific the rubric, the more valid the result; feasibility, however, often demands that we use generic rubrics more often.

• Decisions must be made regarding what constitutes apt evidence of real understanding (as opposed to merely accurate recall, thoughtless use of knowledge, or quantity of information)?

Rubrics can be developed in many ways, ranging from teacher-designed rubrics to those designed by the students. An effective approach is to balance student and teacher input. Maximizing student involvement in the development of rubrics builds ownership for the learning process.

ACTIVITY 12
Setting Criteria Together

Students familiar with the portfolio process gain ownership and understanding of the process when they help set the criteria for preparing and evaluating their portfolios. You may use the following steps to set criteria together.

1. As a class, ask students to brainstorm criteria for portfolio evaluation. As part of the brainstorming session, you can add to the list.

2. Moving into small groups, students work to choose perhaps three or four of the criteria that they want to use for their portfolios. Each group reports their selections to you. As you mark their choices on the original list, you'll likely note that certain criteria are preferred by several of the groups. Criteria with the most "votes" become the criteria for evaluation. You may need to adjust the final list to make it manageable (shorter) and yet long enough to demonstrate learning. Ensure that students understand any necessary changes to the criteria.

3. Assign each small group one criterion and ask them to generate standards of performance (three or four levels are recommended). Sample rubrics (such as those in **Figure 9.2**) and sample rubric vocabulary can ease their task. Sample vocabulary to suggest: rarely, sometimes, always; little use, some use, regular use; limited, partial, comprehensive; none, some, many.

4. Compile a draft of the rubric for the class to review. Changes and refinements may occur as a result of testing and discussing the rubric using work samples.

One example of how to involve students who are familiar with the concept of portfolios is demonstrated in **Activity 12.**

The advantage of a student-involved or student-generated rubric is that the language of the rubric will be owned and understood by the students. **Figure 9.2** contains an example of a rubric which was developed by students in a 10th grade mathematics class. A blank template for developing rubrics is provided in **Appendix M.**

One of the most difficult decisions for a teacher using portfolios is the decision to grade or not to grade portfolios. **Activity 13** (p. 95) is designed to help you consider the variety of perspectives on this issue. Sample responses to that figure appear in **Figure 9.3**, where a high school teacher and a primary teacher share their thoughts about the grading of portfolios.

PRACTICAL APPROACHES TO EVALUATION

Although grading is a controversial issue, portfolios do need to be evaluated in some way.

FIGURE 9.2

Sample Portfolio Evaluation Form

This sample portfolio evaluation form was developed by 10th grade math students.
Use the template in **Appendix M** to draft your own.

Name: _____   Date: _____

Rated by: ☐ Self ☐ Peer_____   ☐ Teacher ☐ Other_____
                                    (name)   (name and relationship)

| | 1 | 2 | 3 | 4 | 5 |

Criteria	Low	Middle	High
Presentation and Visual Appeal Score: _____	• messy writing • not colorful or eye-catching • few or no titles	• neat writing • somewhat colorful or eye-catching • some titles	• very neat writing or types • no unnecessary marks on papers • very colorful or eye-catching • all entries have titles
Organization Score: _____	• poor table of contents (or none) • items not in order according to table of contents • no dates • no letter of introduction	• acceptable table of contents, not everything included • some items out of place • some dates • letter is present, but not specific	• clear table of contents • everything in order • all items are included • follows organization stated in letter of introduction

FIGURE 9.2 (continued)

Variety of Entries	• entries have little or no variety • lots of repetition	• some variety in entries • some repetition	• wide variety of entries • few, if any repetitions
Score: _____			
Growth and Learning Experiences	• unrealistic goals or no goals set • all reflections are stating the same thing—strengths or weaknesses • no corrections made on work • no peer responses	• one or more realistic goals • some variety in reflections • some corrections made on work • some peer responses	• realistic goals • a wide variety of reflections— reflecting strengths and weaknesses • all corrections made • variety of peer responses
Score: _____			

Comments

Total Score: _____

(form adapted from Rolheiser, 1996. Rubrics developed by students in MAT 2A4.20 & MAT 2A4.30 Exeter High School, 1998)

ACTIVITY 13
To Grade or Not to Grade?

Work with a group of your colleagues to share different perspectives on the issue of grading portfolios. You'll need the following materials: 4 signs (Strongly Agree, Agree, Disagree, Strongly Disagree), flip chart paper or overhead transparencies, and markers.

1. Use a four-corners cooperative structure. Post a sign in each corner of the room.
- Corner 1: Strongly Agree
- Corner 2: Agree
- Corner 3: Strongly Disagree
- Corner 4: Disagree

2. Post the following statement for the group: Portfolios should be graded.

3. Ask participants to decide which response they feel most comfortable with and to think about their reasons for making that choice. Give them a few minutes to decide.

4. Ask participants to move to the corner of the room with the response they have chosen, find a partner, and discuss their reasons for choosing that response. Allow 5 minutes for the discussions.

5. The facilitator asks for perspectives from each of the four corners. The norm at this stage is to listen to the varying perspectives without commentary.

6. After each group has shared its perspectives, open the floor to discussion, clarification, and affirmation. Often the facilitator asks for additional information, such as what grades are taught by the participants in each corner.

7. Debriefing should include the following points:
- Your choice to grade or not is influenced by a variety of factors including general beliefs about the purpose of assessment, evaluation, and grading, experiences as a teacher and learner, the practices used in your present class or school, the grade level you teach, external expectations, requirements, and accountability.
- Your choice is not likely to remain static. As experience with the portfolio process is gained, and as changes in your work context occur, your thoughts and choices may alter.
- It is valuable to recognize alternative points of view. Other perspectives promote clear thinking about the pros and cons of your stance and increase your understanding of choices that are made in different contexts and circumstances.

8. Put the following quotation on an overhead and have participants share personal scenarios that illustrate key points in the quotation.

Many educators ask about converting the results of performance assessment to traditional grades. There are no easy answers to this question for the simple reason that the issue of grading does not lend itself to simplistic approaches. The reasons for this difficulty, however, are not related to performance assessment, but to the varied methods and purposes for assigning grades. (Danielson, 1997, p. 17)

Consider the following ideas as you think about evaluating students' portfolios.

Supplying feedback: Students need and want feedback. The research on motivation and learning highlights the need for meaningful feedback as well as knowledge of results. It can be provided orally (e.g., conferences, audiotapes) or in writing (e.g., comments on specific portfolio items, summary comments). A key question is how to provide specific feedback, especially given large classes. One possibility is to provide feedback in writing, since this allows you to do so beyond actual class hours. Another possibility is to design creative scheduling where teachers buddy up classes to allow one teacher time for individual or small group feedback. Large classes also necessitate that the feedback pool is larger than just the teacher (peers feedback becomes essential). Richard Arends (1994, p. 323–325) summarizes important guidelines for providing feedback:

- Provide feedback as soon as possible.
- Make feedback specific.
- Keep feedback appropriate to the developmental stage of the learner.
- Emphasize praise and feedback on correct performance.
- When giving negative feedback, show how to perform correctly.
- Help students to focus on process, rather than outcomes.
- Teach students how to judge their own performances.

If you use these guidelines for thinking about portfolios, some suggestions for actions emerge. For example, individual entries can be regularly responded to by you or by peers either as written peer responses, anecdotal teacher comments, or verbal sharing in carousels (see Chapter 7).

Allotting time for feedback: If most or all entries have been responded to throughout the process, then a summative evaluation won't take much time. If the summative evaluation involves reviewing a fair number of new entries for each student, however, you'll need to allow more time.

Facilitating fair evaluation: For the most effective evaluation by students, peers, and parents, it is imperative that they make judgments before the teacher's evaluation is known. The inherent power associated with the teacher's role may unfairly influence the decisions made by others. For this reason, consider the sequence of evaluations. You can use the evaluations done by others to gain insights into your students' work. Often, these varied insights provide a balanced portrait of the learner.

Facilitating effective evaluation: If portfolios are to be evaluated by people who are new to the process, specific structure and guidelines may need to be provided to help ensure that students receive positive feedback and encouragement to continue working toward identified goals. For example, you can provide appropriate support to students by identifying and commenting on their strengths.

PRACTICAL APPROACHES TO GRADING

Beyond evaluating portfolios, you may also choose to grade them. Below are suggestions for approaching grading.

Four-Level Rubric with Letter Grades: A rubric that provides five levels of performance for each criteria (superior performance, proficient performance, adequate performance, and limited performance), could translate into the following grading system:

   A+   superior performance
   B   proficient performance
   C   adequate performance
   D   limited performance

Four-Level Rubric: A rubric that provides four levels of performance could be assigned points as follows: Superior, 4; Proficient, 3; Adequate, 2;

FIGURE 9.3

Sample Responses to Activity 13 (To Grade or Not to Grade?)

The following responses to **Activity 13** offer ideas that you might find useful in starting conversations and sharing thoughts on the issue of grading student portfolios.

Barb's Ideas

I would place myself in Corner 2, Agree. In an ideal world, grades would not be the primary motivating force behind students' effort and achievement and I would choose not to grade portfolios. In my high school, however, students are highly motivated by grades and they would not put as much thought and effort into their portfolios if these assessments were not part of their final mark. This is not only my opinion—kids have told me this again and again when we review the assessment and evaluation elements of their courses at the end of each semester. I believe in the power of portfolio assessment and its ability to reveal aspects of learners that may not appear on more traditional types of assessments, for example, in tests and homework. It makes sense, therefore, to include portfolios in my overall evaluation and grading of students' skills and efforts. I hope that students value the anecdotal evaluation of their work far more than just the grade on it—some do and some don't. It must be noted that students are not the only participants in the process who value marks; colleagues of mine have also told me quite openly that they would not devote much time to portfolio assessment if it were not part of their students' final grades.

Some day I hope that students will come to me having had lots of experience with portfolios, and that they will be motivated to continue developing them whether or not these assessments are graded. Until that time, however, in my setting, portfolios will be graded.

Shari's Ideas

My current position on the issue of grading portfolios is that I disagree with the practice (Corner 4). As a preservice teacher required to develop and maintain a professional portfolio, however, I undoubtedly benefited from the extrinsic motivation of knowing that my cross-curricular portfolio would be graded. Having struggled with the initial phases of the process, it is unlikely that I would have continued to put forth as great an effort had a final grade not been assigned. Much to my surprise, the process became a powerful tool for encouraging not only academic achievement, but personal growth as well. My later portfolio entries were intrinsically motivated and more a labor of love than a desire for an A.

As a 2nd grade teacher and former kindergarten teacher, I really have had no need or desire to grade my students' portfolios. In contrast to my preservice teaching experience, it is my belief that grades are of little interest to most primary students and are not likely to serve as strong motivators. The student growth I have witnessed since commencing portfolio assessment in my classrooms has been significant. I have observed many young children reflect on their learning and clearly articulate their strengths, areas for growth, and achievement over time. Valuing and assessing student effort and achievement are important at all grade levels; grading, however, is not essential for successful implementation of the portfolio process in my present context.

Limited, 1. For each criteria a score of 0 to 4 is assigned. These numbers are totaled and converted to an overall percentage.

Percentage Values: Assign each level of performance a range of percentage values: Superior, 90–100; Proficient, 70–89; Adequate, 50–69; Limited, 0–49.

For each of the previous examples of levels of performance, teachers, students, parents, or peers should be able to use the rubric for evaluation. The teacher can determine final grades while considering input from some or all of these individuals if this practice is permissible in your environment. Whether you assign weight to the responses by other evaluators can be determined by your level of confidence and your experience with sharing evaluation decisions with others. For example, teachers just beginning to use portfolios often want their own evaluation to count the most in determining a final grade. Issues of control and power over grading are challenging ones that all teachers struggle with, but growth in confidence and experience often results in greater comfort in initiating grading partnerships. The most important consideration is that everyone knows his role and how the portfolio will be evaluated and graded.

The generic rubric in **Figure 9.4** and the specific rubric in **Figure 9.5** illustrate what various levels of performance could be for sample criteria. These can be easily adapted for a variety of purposes. **Figure 9.6** is an example of a letter to students that outlines final requirements for portfolio evaluation.

As you review the decisions from the activities in this chapter, record them on the form in **Planner I** for later review. Based on new information and new facets of the portfolio process, you may want to revise earlier decisions. Your philosophy about evaluation and grading may remain static, change slightly, or even alter dramatically. Naturally, your school culture may influence your evaluation and grading practices.

FIGURE 9.4

Generic Rubric for Portfolio Evaluation

The following generic portfolio evaluation rubric can be adapted to fit your needs.

Student's Name: _____ Date: _____ Evaluated by: _____

	Superior (90-100%)	Proficient (70-89%)	Adequate (50-69%)	Limited (under 50%)
	Level 4	Level 3	Level 2	Level 1
Variety	• contains a wide variety of work	• contains some variety of work	• contains little variety of work	• contains no variety of work
Organization	• clearly organized	• organized	• somewhat organized	• disorganized
Communication	• clear communication of ideas	• some ideas are communicated clearly	• few ideas are communicated clearly	• no ideas are communicated clearly
Evidence of Understanding	• shows real understanding	• shows some understanding	• shows little understanding	• shows no understanding
Self-Assessment	• evidence of thorough, realistic and constructive self-assessment	• evidence of realistic self-assessment	• little evidence of realistic self-assessment	• self-assessment does not correspond to performance

Comments	Final Evaluation
	☐ 4 – Superior (90-100%)
	☐ 3 – Proficient (70-89%)
	☐ 2 – Adequate (50-69%)
	☐ 1 – Limited (under 50%)

FIGURE 9.5

Specific Rubric for Portfolio Evaluation

This specific rubric illustrates various levels of performance for sample criteria. Use this as an example to draft your own criteria and rubric. When you evaluate the whole portfolio, use the blank column for comments.

Student's Name:_____

PORTFOLIO		Comments	
Introduction and Synthesis	All areas of introduction are completed, thoughtfully and carefully. Synthesis is completed thoughtfully and carefully.		☐ Superior Achievement ☐ Proficient Achievement ☐ Adequate Achievement ☐ Limited Achievement ☐ Achievement not Demonstrated
Goal Statement	Thoughtful, relevant goal statement completed.		☐ Superior Achievement ☐ Proficient Achievement ☐ Adequate Achievement ☐ Limited Achievement ☐ Achievement not Demonstrated
Organization	Portfolio is well organized, according to date, subject area, multiple intelligence or other appropriate means. Entries are easy to find.		☐ Superior Achievement ☐ Proficient Achievement ☐ Adequate Achievement ☐ Limited Achievement ☐ Achievement not Demonstrated

FIGURE 9.5 (continued)		
PORTFOLIO (continued)	Comments	
Entries	At least 15 entries from this school year. Entries show evidence of challenges, growth, and personal pride. Reflections are thoughtful, describe what entry is about, explain reason for inclusion in portfolio and reflect on what was learned. Peer responses are from a variety of different people.	☐ Superior Achievement ☐ Proficient Achievement ☐ Adequate Achievement ☐ Limited Achievement ☐ Achievement not Demonstrated
Neatness and Presentation	Portfolio is neat and tidy. Spelling, grammar, and punctuation are attended to in reflections.	☐ Superior Achievement ☐ Proficient Achievement ☐ Adequate Achievement ☐ Limited Achievement ☐ Achievement not Demonstrated
Responses to Peers	Responds to a variety of class peers. Responses show evidence of thought, consideration, and offer constructive feedback.	☐ Superior Achievement ☐ Proficient Achievement ☐ Adequate Achievement ☐ Limited Achievement ☐ Achievement not Demonstrated

FIGURE 9.5 (continued)		
INTERVIEW	Comments	
Knowledge of Portfolio	Knows what is in portfolio. Finds entries easily. Thinks about which entry to choose.	☐ Superior Achievement ☐ Proficient Achievement ☐ Adequate Achievement ☐ Limited Achievement ☐ Achievement not Demonstrated
Learning Experience	Identifies key learning experiences. Explains relevance of learning experiences to self. Makes appropriate choices.	☐ Superior Achievement ☐ Proficient Achievement ☐ Adequate Achievement ☐ Limited Achievement ☐ Achievement not Demonstrated
Presentation	Shows confidence, speaks clearly. Shows entries to highlight presentation. Answers questions without a lot of prompting.	☐ Superior Achievement ☐ Proficient Achievement ☐ Adequate Achievement ☐ Limited Achievement ☐ Achievement not Demonstrated

(adapted with permission from W. Hunsburger, 1998)

FIGURE 9.6

Letter to Students

To help your students achieve a clear understanding of how the portfolios will be evaluated, you may find it useful to adapt the following letter. A letter gives both the students and the teacher a concrete beginning for understanding, facilitates discussion, and serves as a reference point.

Dear Students:

The final assessment of your portfolio will consist of the following components.

(1) A portfolio interview with the teacher and a small group of your peers.

(2) A written introduction to your portfolio including a synthesis of what your portfolio shows about you.

(3) A review of your portfolio by the teacher.

Interview

Your interview will occur during the week of _____. You will be interviewed with 2 or 3 of your peers. You may invite your parents to this interview.

You should be prepared to present the highlights of your portfolio and to discuss some of the important things you have learned this year.

The interview will last from 5 to 10 minutes. Interviews will occur during class time. A schedule will be posted by _____.

Portfolio Introduction

Please prepare an introduction that reflects your entire portfolio. You may use the sheet provided or create your own. In your introduction be sure to include information on how your portfolio is organized, what you are particularly proud of, and anything special you want a reviewer to notice. You should also include your goals for next year.

In addition to this basic introduction, select 3–5 entries that you feel best show who you are as a student. Try to choose entries that cover different subjects and different times of the school year (they should not all be from one term). Give your reasons for choosing these entries and explain what they show about you and how they show it.

Final Review

Your finished portfolio is due on _____. There are no extensions.

Your portfolio will be assessed using the same criteria that were used for previous reviews. A copy of the portfolio evaluation rubric is attached.

Grading

Your portfolio grade will be ___% of your final grade.

(adapted with permission from W. Hunsburger, 1998)

After working through the activities in Chapter 9, use this form to record your decisions.

1. Review the criteria that you selected in Chapter 3 (see **Planner C**). Record these below, making adjustments if you choose.

2. Who will develop the rubric for evaluation?
   ☐ Teacher
   ☐ Teacher and colleagues
   ☐ Teacher and students

3. How many levels of performance are desired for the evaluation rubric?
   ☐ Three
   ☐ Four
   ☐ Five

4. How will levels of performance be determined? What process will be used to identify or develop these levels of performance?

5. Will the portfolio be graded?
   ☐ Yes
   ☐ No
   ☐ Uncertain

6. Who will be involved in the grading process?
   ☐ Students
   ☐ Peers
   ☐ Parents
   ☐ Teacher
   ☐ _____

7. How will the grading be determined (e.g., percentages, letter grades)?

8. How will the portfolio grade be incorporated into the overall grading scheme for the student?

GETTING STARTED WITH STUDENTS

KEY IDEAS

- Introduce and explore collections as a preface to portfolios
- How to devise the first portfolio entry
- Practical tips

OVERVIEW

This chapter contains ideas that range from ways to make you feel comfortable with the overall concept of portfolio assessment to practical ways of introducing portfolios to students of all ages and experiences. Use the ideas and activities to help articulate your practices for interested partners, including administrators, parents, and students. In addition, one teacher's story of her initial experiences with portfolio assessment illustrates the intricacies of the process.

DEVELOP AN UNDERSTANDING OF PORTFOLIOS

Your confidence in understanding what portfolios are and why they are important in your classroom as a teaching and assessment tool is critical to introducing portfolios to your students. Meet with colleagues and use **Activity 14** to increase every-

one's knowledge and comfort with the concept of portfolio assessment; you can adapt and use it also with upper elementary or older students to introduce them to the concept of portfolios. If a video or similar activity is not available or practical in your setting, review column 2 of **Activity 14** as a reminder of why portfolios are valuable.

Most students are familiar with collecting things—if you ask them, you'll find that many have collections of rocks, sports cards, or souvenirs from field trips and vacations. Initially, you can build on their understanding of collections by drawing an analogy between collections and portfolios. In the case of portfolios, students collect their work. Later in the process you can help students take steps to select, focus, and reflect on their work to make the collection a complete portfolio. The following suggestions for how to introduce the concept of portfolios to your students builds on their knowledge of collections.

INTRODUCE A COLLECTIONS UNIT

An extremely effective way to introduce the concept of portfolios to students of all ages is to begin with the idea of a collection. The adapted activity on the next page (in conversation with Shari Schwartz, 1998) is designed for young children but can be easily modified for older students.

ACTIVITY 14
Why Use Portfolios?

Use this video activity to clarify the important characteristics of portfolio assessment and to explore the reasons for using portfolios in your teaching.

A Video Introduction to Portfolio Assessment

Choosing a facilitator simplifies the process of the following activity.

1. Participants choose a partner. One partner is given the question "What is a portfolio?" The other partner is given the question, "Why use portfolios?" (Allow 5 minutes.)

2. The facilitator loads the video *Redesigning Assessment: Portfolios* (ASCD, 1992) and asks everyone to take notes on the information that may pertain to answering the questions. The facilitator can offer participants a copy of **Activity 15** to help focus the activity.
The group views the first part of the video (about 15 minutes).

3. At the end of the first part of the video, partners interview each other and record the ideas generated for each of the questions. (Allow about 10 minutes for discussion.)

4. The facilitator leads a discussion with the whole group while participants record additional ideas. The facilitator may summarize the discussion, referring to the definition and ideas in this activity.

5. Partners conclude the activity by discussing their most compelling reasons for initiating portfolio assessment. (Allow about 5 minutes.)

Key Portfolio Points

A portfolio is a purposeful collection of student work that exhibits the student's efforts, progress, and achievements in one or more areas. The collection must include student participation in selecting contents, the criteria for selection, the criteria for judging merit, and evidence of student self-reflection.

—*F. L. Paulson, P. R. Paulson, and C. A. Meyer (1991, p. 60)*

What Is a Portfolio?
• a purposeful collection of student work that exhibits students' efforts, progress, achievements, and reflection
• a comprehensive record of growth and development
• a process that involves learners at every stage

Why Use Portfolios?
• to encourage self-directed learning
• to enlarge the view of what is learned
• to foster learning about learning
• to demonstrate progress toward goals
• to provide a window into students' heads and hearts
• to intersect instruction and assessment
• to provide a vehicle for students to value themselves as learners
• to offer opportunities for peer-supported growth

ACTIVITY 15
Three-Step Interview

Offer participants this form as you work through **Activity 14**. Participants can take notes from the video on this form and add information gathered from the group discussion. Notes are useful for reminders and later review.

1. Partner 1: What is a portfolio?

2. Partner 2: Why use portfolios?

3. List key group ideas:

-

-

-

-

-

-

-

Introduce a collections unit to your class.

1. Talk about collections with your students; create class collections, bring in your own collection, invite other adults to share their collections with the class, and have students bring in things that they collect.

2. Discuss the idea of a collection so that children become comfortable with language associated with collecting. Ask questions such as these: "What are your favorite items in your collection?" "What does your collection show about you?" "Which item isn't your favorite? Why?"

3. Have students practice asking visitors these questions so that they develop vocabulary associated with a collection.

4. Initiate a booklet for the class. In that booklet, assign each student a page and a specific pattern to follow. For example, [Matthew] collects [patches]. [His] favorite part of the collection is [the lobster patch from Maine]. [Matthew] has about [25 patches] in [his] collection.

Alternatively, ask each student to write a sentence or a paragraph that describes a collection (either real or imaginary). Ask the student to illustrate the page.

5. As students work with collections, they will become comfortable with the major concepts of collecting materials and thinking critically about the attributes of those materials. At this point, the idea of a portfolio as a collection of their school work and learning can be introduced. Their experience with a collections unit helps to prepare them for making judgments about which pieces of work they will include in their portfolios.

Help students understand the concept of a portfolio.

1. As whole-class activity, brainstorm examples of different types of collections. For example, a photo collection in an album, a hope chest, a toy chest, and an artist's portfolio are all types of collections.

2. Ask students, "What is it about those things

that made you list them?" Students often respond that they chose things that have something in common, that are meaningful to them, or represent special places that they've visited.

3. Ask the students to cluster, group, or categorize items based on common or similar criteria attributes (e.g., family photos and photos of friends, inherited family items, and gifts from friends).

4. Based on the knowledge that a portfolio is a type of collection, ask students how they would define a portfolio. If your students are stumped, ask them "What is the essence of a portfolio?" As a group, you may work toward an answer similar to "a portfolio is a collection of things gathered over time that have meaning for and reflect personal values of the owner."

5. Discuss issues related to portfolios and collections. The following issues may arise as a result of the discussion:

    a. Evolution: What is the period of time over which a particular collection has been developed?

    b. Voice and choice: Whose voice and choice are being reflected in the collection?

    c. Audience: Who will be looking at this? How will it be shared?

6. Summarize the activity by emphasizing that no single process leads to a portfolio. Each person shapes individual process, although sometimes teachers or others structure the process and help students move from one step to the next.

STRUCTURE A FIRST ENTRY AND PEER RESPONSE

One way to ensure student excitement about and interest in using portfolio assessment is to carefully structure the first entry. A good place to start is by choosing a learning experience that you know successfully engages students. Use that experience to introduce portfolio assessment. For example, you might begin the school year by preparing students to write and illustrate a picture book with the theme "All About Me." The first lesson can be an exploratory look at a range of children's picture books. A series of structured group and individual tasks engages the learners in exploring these books for themes, artistic techniques, and layout formats. The learners look at how an author engages the reader, as well as how the author determines the focus for the story. The second lesson introduces the students to a range of illustration techniques and gives them an opportunity to experiment with some of those techniques. The students are then given an outline sheet for the book and have about two weeks to complete their book. On the due date they share the book by reading it aloud to a small group of peers, who offer oral feedback. The oral feedback can be structured as follows:

- One thing I liked about your book is _____ because _____.
- One question I have is: _____?

Once all group members, perhaps four students in each group, complete the sharing task, students are paired within the group. Give them a sheet to record their answers to the following prompts.

- What did you learn from this experience?
- How did you grow or change?

The partners share their answers and they both write a peer response (see **Appendix E**). The written components are quite successful because each student has had the opportunity to think about and verbalize answers and ideas.

At the end of the lesson, you can tell the students that they have completed their first portfolio entry and that they will learn about portfolios the next day. The activity is a successful beginning to the portfolio process because

- All students can be successful.

- The activity has the capacity to generate a lot of pride, which encourages students to continue the process.
- Peer sharing in small groups allows for a safe start and facilitates risk taking and public sharing, factors that are essential to the next steps in the process.

REVIEW SAMPLE PORTFOLIOS

It is enormously beneficial for both students and teachers to review samples of student portfolios early in the process. Experienced teachers often keep samples of students' portfolios because they offer a rich portrait of the similarities and differences among different portfolio assessment models. Portfolios kept by students of different ages can be particularly valuable to compare and contrast because certain aspects of them may be common to all ages, while others are quite different depending on the age and experience of the students.

Teachers and students may record their ideas as they review the sample portfolios. If portfolio samples are organized at different stations, then the students may use **Appendix N** to record their thoughts. If participants are sitting in groups and viewing a variety of portfolios, ask students to use a form similar to the one in **Activity 16**. In either case, a whole class discussion about what they've reviewed and what they realistically plan to achieve can stimulate ideas and excitement about portfolios.

TIPS AND DIPS

The following tips are designed to help you and your students begin to use portfolios successfully.

- *Start small.* To achieve manageability and to ensure success for you and your students, think big, but start small. For instance, try using portfolios with only one class, starting with only one subject, or choosing to focus on your favorite area of the curriculum.

ACTIVITY 16
Comparing Sample Portfolios

With a partner, examine samples of student portfolios. Use the table below to identify key similarities and differences among grade levels and models. Use the analysis to help target key areas for your students to focus on when developing their portfolios.

Similarities	Differences

• *Review critical dates to set up tentative time lines.* You need to have a general sense of the long-term picture, while realizing that flexibility regarding details of the time lines may be necessary. By outlining key dates, you can set targets to guide your decision making and monitoring of the process. Be sure to take into consideration grading periods and the school calendar (including holidays and testing).

• *Inform parents early in the process about the concept and time lines.* Portfolio assessment is a collaborative process involving many partners; parents are key partners. To ensure that parents understand and can participate in the portfolio process, early and ongoing communication is essential.

• *A first portfolio entry is often "about me."* The first entry a student prepares for the portfolio often introduces something interesting about the student. A personalized entry promotes success because it is usually easy for students to document something unique about themselves. A first entry does not replace the introductory letter, which is usually written at the end of the portfolio process.

• *Remember that goal setting must occur early and be revisited periodically throughout the term.* Initial goal setting is an important step. Keep one copy of each student's recorded goal or goals in the portfolio and another in your files. Periodically structure time for students to revisit their goals and to evaluate their progress toward those goals.

• *Use different colors of paper for various forms.* A specific color of paper for each standard form (e.g., table of contents and reflection sheets) can help you quickly find the form you need. If you and your students are using the same evaluation rubric, for example, you'll know at a glance that the student's evaluation is on blue paper and yours is on yellow. Using different colors of paper can simplify organizing and managing several aspects of students' portfolios.

• *Administer pretests before you have the students begin portfolios.* Items such as attitude surveys, social skills checklists, and sample audiotapes of students' reading can become powerful entries if comparative data is provided by posttests. Both pretests and posttests can be included in the final portfolio. These before-and-after assessments can provide valuable information that demonstrates a child's growth in one or more areas.

• *Set up an area in the classroom where portfolio materials are readily available.* Materials such as reflection sheets, a date stamp, and a stapler should be readily available to students if they are expected to independently create a portfolio entry and track and organize their own learning.

• *Be flexible about unusual entries in students' portfolios.* Nearly any artifact from home that a child feels passionate about, for example, may be appropriate for that child's language arts portfolio—as long as the student includes a reflection piece.

• *Practice using the "language of reflection" at the beginning of the portfolio process.* Children need to observe modeling and have opportunities for practice to become comfortable with the language of reflection. Using prompts (e.g., I like this piece of work because . . .) and providing a lot of modeling using the students' own work helps them become comfortable with using appropriate language.

• *Look forward to the realization "that achieving clarity, skill, and commitment is a progressive process"* (Bennett, Rolheiser, & Stevahn, 1991, p. 338). As you explore and experiment, expect to be challenged. It is by grappling with such challenges that you become clear about your goals, develop skill in managing the process, and build commitment to collaborative assessment practices. Working through challenges results in powerful learning for you and your students.

Decision making occurs constantly in any educational process, especially in the implementation of portfolios. In **Figure 10.1**, a teacher shares her thoughts and decisions as she worked through the implementation of portfolio assessment in her classroom.

Early decisions about criteria and the type of portfolio can influence later decisions about evaluating the final product. Moreover, decisions made later in the portfolio process can alter earlier decisions, such as whether to grade the portfolios. The age of students, their experiences, and school culture are just a few of the factors that influence decision making. As you think about your first steps, consider these questions: (1) How will you introduce portfolios to your students? (2) Which tips from this chapter do you most want to keep in mind? (3) What elements of Laurel's story (**Figure 10.1**) may be helpful to you?

FIGURE 10.1

A Teacher's Story

I decided to try portfolios in my 6th grade classroom. I made the following decisions based on the needs of my students and the requirements of the programs in my school and district. My story illustrates some of my preplanning, as well as decisions we made as implementation progressed. —*Laurel*

Purpose, Type, Audiences, and Time Frame

• I wanted my students to think critically and creatively, to engage in teamwork productively, and to be motivated to pursue personal goals.

• My purpose for using portfolio assessment: To provide as many opportunities as possible for my students to practice skills and to achieve their goals.

• The portfolios are primarily Best Work collections because I felt that this was a familiar starting point for my students.

• Two pieces that showed *improvement* in writing were to be included as part of the collection because I feel it is important to have students show some growth along with their best work.

• The students share their portfolios with classmates and me.

• The portfolios were maintained over an entire year.

Getting Started

• I wanted students to keep all of their writing assignments so that they would have a base collection of work from which to choose initial portfolio entries.

• I introduced the idea of portfolios by conducting a lesson on collections in general (e.g., baseball cards, teddy bears, and coins) and having students bring their collections to class to share with their peers.

• I sent a letter home to parents to let them know that their children were creating portfolios.

Categories for Entries

• The portfolios focus on writing: Students included samples of short stories, persuasive essays, poetry, and research reports.

Learning Expectations and Criteria

• I discussed with students what was important for good writing. After considering their input, I chose four major criteria for their selection of best work: good mechanics, creativity, variety of entries, and clear communication of ideas.

A First Entry and Reflection

• I modeled a work sample and reflection from my own professional portfolio.

• Students chose their own learning sample and wrote a reflection for it, after receiving some sample starters for the reflection.

Storing and Organizing Portfolios

• Students used three-ring binders as their portfolio containers. The binders were manageable and practical because my classroom space was limited.

• Students were encouraged to decorate the binders with symbols and illustrations that were meaningful to them.

• As learning samples were chosen and reflections created, the completed entries were listed in a Table of Contents at the front of the binder, with columns listing the date of entry, title of entry, category of writing, and the audience.

Sharing the Learning

• Students began sharing their entries by participating in a show-and-tell process in their cooperative groups.

• Show and tell extended into exchanging written peer responses using sample starters.

• I responded to certain entries chosen by the students.

• Eventually I hope my students can conduct conferences with their parents.

I plan for that step to happen after we have gained experience with portfolios.

Goal Setting

• Students chose two goals for their writing. One goal is related to mechanics and the other is related to originality or creativity.

• Goals were established after the portfolio process was started. I met briefly with each student about personal goals.

• Goals were revisited at the end of the portfolio process. We shared anecdotal feedback about whether the goals had been reached.

Evaluation and Grading

• Because I have many concerns about the pros and cons of grading the portfolios, I decided not to grade them this year. I felt that the process was meaningful because of the authentic purpose in sharing entries and the entire portfolio with others (both within my class and with younger students in other classes).

• My students knew at the beginning of the process that the construction of a portfolio was a requirement for passing the class.

My Ideas for the Future

• As I review the decisions and plans I have made, I wonder how I will develop the reflective capacity of my students. I want to think more about this component.

• I will meet with colleagues who have tried using portfolios and do more professional reading to gather ideas for future use.

STARTING A PROFESSIONAL PORTFOLIO

KEY IDEAS

- Rationale for maintaining professional portfolios
- Exploring a range of purposes, types, and audiences
- Categories for entries
- Work and learning samples
- Reflections
- Storing and organizing your portfolio
- Sharing the learning
- Goal setting
- Self-evaluation

OVERVIEW

What are the benefits of maintaining a professional portfolio? How do you start? These and many other questions about professional portfolios are addressed in this chapter. As you work through the ideas, you'll see the correlation between the elements of a student's portfolio and the necessary components of your own portfolio.

RATIONALE FOR PROFESSIONAL PORTFOLIOS

Educators in many countries are beginning to document their work as a means of portraying who they are as professionals. As an educator, you are on a continuum of growth beginning with your preservice experiences and continuing throughout your career. If you are a teacher candidate, maintaining a portfolio beginning with your preservice teacher education program can powerfully document both your growth and performance as a new professional. Your portfolio may be used as an evaluative tool in the teacher education program, especially if it is targeted to specific learning expectations and goals, and it can be a valuable asset as you seek employment. For experienced teachers, the process of maintaining a portfolio provides focus for continuing professional development and lifelong learning; it can be used for advancement, performance review, and self-assessment. Additionally, the process and the product can be exceptionally affirming. Ultimately, a professional portfolio helps you to celebrate the successes and challenges of your career.

FIRST STEPS

Your first steps in developing a professional portfolio can be a formal or informal professional development experience. If an external body mandates the use of professional portfolios, effective professional development should be designed to assist you in starting and maintaining the process. For small or informal groups, use this book and the following practical ideas to help you gather information about professional portfolios:

- Read about professional portfolios.

• Explore the Internet to find information about portfolios.

• Attend a workshop, conference, or institute focusing on portfolios.

• Transfer knowledge gained from using portfolios with students to developing a professional portfolio.

• Form a study group to share information and ideas.

• Review samples of professional portfolios.

• Invite a speaker from another profession to highlight the pros and cons of professional portfolios at a teacher meeting.

• Review sample entries from diverse professional portfolios.

• Use the expertise of a new teacher who has maintained a professional portfolio in a teacher preparation program. Ask the new teacher to guide everyone in learning about portfolios.

• Learn with others by asking staff members to bring in evidence of new learning. Schedule a meeting (or add activities to the agenda of a staff meeting), or meet in pairs, to share samples and personal reflections. Afterward, ask each person to prepare a written reflection.

• Collect a range of learning samples (e.g., detailed lesson or unit plans, student products, written curriculum). Review these samples and determine criteria that may suit your needs or match samples to predetermined criteria.

• View a video on authentic assessment or portfolio assessment.

• Interview a partner about a meaningful professional experience. Record key reflections. Attach a professional work sample that represents your learning. For example, you may choose a lesson plan, a handout from a professional development session you conducted, or an outline for a community project you are convening.

• At a staff meeting, ask each person to generate and record a brief description of a recent professional experience that was a source of pride, achievement, or significant growth. Choose one word that describes the experience and then share the word with the whole group. Select a partner to interview about the professional experience.

Another option for exploring professional portfolios is to complete **Activity 17**, which focuses on generating personal and professional samples that represent accomplishments. You may use **Appendix O** to record the discussion from **Activity 17**.

EXPLORING A RANGE OF PURPOSES, TYPES, AND AUDIENCES

As with a student portfolio, the first step in creating a professional portfolio is to establish the purpose or purposes for the portfolio. Your portfolio may be designed to help you

• Demonstrate standards of practice (e.g., for evaluation or certification by a College of Teachers)

• Prepare for a performance review or external evaluation

• Gain employment

• Pursue advancement (e.g., a leadership position)

• Make a career change

• Change roles within the profession

• Enhance professional growth

• Perform self-assessment and self-directed learning

The purpose of a professional portfolio influences the type of portfolio. If the purpose of the portfolio is to gain employment or prepare for an external evaluation, for example, a best work portfolio that showcases exemplary work samples is the best choice. If the purpose is to target and develop professional goals, however, a growth portfolio is appropriate. A growth portfolio allows you to demonstrate progress toward identified goals and to highlight your accomplishments as you work toward those goals.

ACTIVITY 17
Time Capsule

Use this activity to focus on personal and professional samples that represent your accomplishments. You can think of the samples as items you might put in a time capsule. The samples should capture growth and achievement, personally and professionally. Select a facilitator before the meeting to give that person time to prepare for modeling answers. Use **Appendix O** to record the discussion.

1. Ask participants to choose a partner.

2. The facilitator introduces the fundamental reasons for having the meeting and then shares one personal and two professional artifacts that would be appropriate for a time capsule. The samples should capture growth and achievement.

3. After that experience, the partners meet together. Partner 1 asks Partner 2 to identify three artifacts that best represent him, as an individual and as a professional. These artifacts could be items that reflect a source of pride, growth, achievement, or importance to the individual.

4. Partner 2 records the three items on the recording sheet.

5. Partners change roles and Partner 2 asks Partner 1 the questions; Partner 1 records the responses.

6. Partners interview each other about items selected and reasons for their selections.

7. If time allows, ask two sets of partners to meet together. The original partners introduce each other to the foursome by relating something interesting about that person's professional achievements.

8. Large-group debriefing: What were some of the reasons artifacts were selected? What did you think or feel as you were sharing your items with your partner? How is a time capsule like a portfolio?

CATEGORIES FOR ENTRIES: IDENTIFYING POSSIBILITIES

To ensure a focused and organized portfolio, you need to identify and define categories of learning. How are portfolio categories identified? If your portfolio is required by an external source, the categories may be determined for you. For example, if you apply for a new teaching position, focus on the criteria outlined on that particular job posting. You might want to construct a best work or show-case portfolio with categories targeted to the criteria listed in the posting:

1. expertise and experience with technology and science,

2. expertise with current instructional strategies,

3. commitment to professional development,

4. experience with team planning, community involvement and school leadership

(Durham District School Board, Posting #211, January 27, 1998).

If the categories are not predetermined, you can choose your own categories. Determine your categories by examining your professional strengths and interests, as well as the nature of the learning and work samples that you have collected.

The categories form the organizational basis for your portfolio. The following categories were developed at the Ontario Institute for Studies in Education of the University of Toronto:

Diversity. Working with all students in an equitable, effective, and caring manner by respecting diversity in relation to ethnicity, race, gender, and special needs of each learner.

Curriculum, Instruction, and Assessment. Developing and applying knowledge of curriculum, instruction, principles of learning, the use of technology, and evaluation needed to implement and monitor effective and evolving programs for all learners.

Ethics and Legalities. Appreciating and practicing the principles, ethics, and legal responsibilities of teaching as a profession.

Active Learner. Being active learners who continuously seek, assess, apply, and communicate knowledge as reflective practitioners throughout their careers.

Collaboration. Initiating, valuing, and practicing collaboration and partnerships with students, colleagues, parents, community, government, and social and business agencies.

Philosophy. Developing a personal philosophy of teaching which is informed by and contributes to the organizational, community, societal, and global contexts of education.

—*Ontario Institute for Studies in Education of the University of Toronto, 1995*

If you choose a growth portfolio, for example, you can focus on any one of those categories for the entire year. Next, identify specific goals and action plans to target all or part of that category and collect evidence to show growth toward the goal. Alternatively, these categories could provide a framework for professional growth over several years. Additional categories are listed in **Figure 11.1**. The categories are given in a variety of groupings to help clarify your thinking about what best suits your purposes.

WORK AND LEARNING SAMPLES

Selecting learning and work samples is a meaningful and engaging part of the portfolio process. As you make selections, consider how they meet the purpose of your portfolio, the identified categories, and your overall goals. Choose a variety of samples that reflect your individuality.

There are many different ways to collect samples. One of the most effective is to regularly select samples and reflect on them in a timely manner—then you're not overwhelmed at the end of the process, you don't forget particular components, and you can review reflections with fresh eyes later. Another method is to maintain a large collection of samples that you can cull and reflect on at a later date. Learning styles and preferences usually determine the type of samples that you select, the approach you use for reflections, and, in turn, the way that entries are organized. A sample is often chosen because it

• Reflects a source of pride and accomplishment.

• Fulfills a requirement set by the organization in which you work or by an external body.

• Meets an expectation, goal, outcome, or standard identified by you or others.

• Represents or exemplifies your growth and achievement or the growth and achievement of your students.

• Highlights a critical event or experience in your professional life.

• Demonstrates your emerging or shifting philosophy of teaching and learning.

• Represents a meaningful experience.

• Illustrates your capacity to inquire, analyze, collaborate, or reflect.

Whereas the choice of each artifact is significant in its own right, the total collection of work and learning samples should form a coherent portrait of you as a professional. Use **Activity 18** to help you create this portrait.

THE IMPORTANCE OF REFLECTIONS AND TECHNIQUES

To understand the importance of reflection in your portfolio, examine its role in a broader educational context. In the late 1980s there was a surge of interest in reflective approaches, both in the preparation of new teachers (Fisher, Fox, & Paille, 1996) and in the enhancement of teachers' professional judgment (Sprinthall, Reiman, Thies-Sprinthall, 1996). This trend was fueled by interest in the cognitive aspects of teachers' decision making and planning, movement toward teacher empowerment, and the increased acceptance of action research and ethnographic inquiry (Fisher, Fox, & Paille, 1996). As described by Sprinthall, Reiman, and Thies-Sprinthall (1996), several bodies of research have contributed to an understanding of reflective thinking; many educators have been affected by their exposure to *The Reflective*

FIGURE 11.1

Categories for Professional Portfolios

If your portfolio is mandated by an external source, your categories may be predetermined. If not, the following groupings of categories may help you consider ideas for your own portfolio.

A. Commitment to students and student learning
Professional Knowledge
Teaching Practice
Leadership and Community
Ongoing Professional Learning

—*Ontario College of Teachers, 1999*

B. Contributions to school success
Planning for instruction and
  assessment
Learning environment
Teaching and learning strategies
Assessment and evaluation of
  student achievement
Interpersonal skills and attitudes

—*Hunsburger, 1998*

C. Curriculum
Instructional skills and strategies
Cocurricular activities
Collaboration
Inquiry
Leadership

D. Theory and research
Practice

E. Development of technical repertoire
Collaboration
Inquiry
Reflective practice

—*Fullan, Bennett, and Rolheiser-Bennett, 1990*

F. Planning and preparation
Classroom environment
Instruction
Professional responsibilities

G. Personal beliefs and philosophy
Professional goals
Curriculum knowledge
Instructional practices
Assessment and evaluation
Collaboration
Professional development

H. Organizational skills
Time management skills
Instructional knowledge, skills, and
  strategies
Collaborative skills
Educational philosophy

ACTIVITY 18
Selecting Work and Learning Samples

Use this activity to focus on your learning and selecting work samples that represent your growth as a professional. Begin by examining the samples listed under the six categories below. Working with a partner, what additional samples can you generate based on your own professional experiences?

1. Diversity: Working with all students in an equitable, effective, and caring manner by respecting diversity in relation to ethnicity, race, gender, and special needs of each learner.
- lesson modifications for exceptional students
- review of texts and classroom materials for bias
- adapted materials for English as Second Language students (e.g., graphic organizers)

2. Curriculum, Instruction, and Assessment: Developing and applying knowledge of curriculum, instruction, principles of learning, the use of technology, and evaluation needed to implement and monitor effective and evolving programs for all learners.
- design of long-range curriculum plans that specify learning expectations
- videotaped lessons demonstrating use of effective instructional strategies (e.g., cooperative learning, inductive thinking, inquiry, simulation)
- use of new assessment practices with students (e.g., portfolio assessment, rubrics, observation checklists)

3. Ethics and Legalities: Appreciating and practicing the principles, ethics, and legal responsibilities of teaching as a profession.
- a colleague or administrator's evaluation of your professionalism
- an analysis of district policy regarding specific extracurricular activities (e.g., field trips)
- a case study analysis of ethical issues

4. Active Learner: Being active learners who continuously seek, assess, apply and communicate knowledge as reflective practitioners throughout their careers.
- a log of key insights gained as a result of attending a conference or institute
- a critique of a current professional article, chapter, or book
- a newsletter article written for a professional organization or school

5. Collaboration: Initiating, valuing, and practicing collaboration and partnerships with students, colleagues, parents, community, government, and social and business agencies.
- a unit or lesson outline codeveloped with a team teaching partner
- videotapes or audiotapes of student-led conferencing
- correspondence with other educators via the Internet

6. Philosophy: Developing a personal philosophy of teaching which is informed by and contributes to the organizational, community, societal and global contexts of education.
- a statement of beliefs regarding teaching and learning
- a school improvement project or plan with underlying rationale articulated
- a multimedia presentation of the school's educational innovations for the community

(Categories from Ontario Institute for Studies in Education of the University of Toronto, 1995)

Practitioner (Schon, 1987), in which the author argues that professional growth, artistry, and competence are framed by an individual's ability to think about what he is doing while doing it.

A second body of professional literature comes from the information-processing line of inquiry (Joyce & Weil, 1996; Bruning, Schraw, & Ronning, 1995), which includes how thinking is organized, the role of meaning in learning, and the cognitive strategies used in problem solving. Many studies focus on the capacity of expert teachers to cluster understandings regarding the teaching and learning process; clustering allows them to retrieve information quickly and to relate it to new knowledge. The process of reflecting and making connections, which is inherent to the portfolio process, contributes to the development of these cognitive strategies.

What emerges from the research described above, and in other preservice and inservice teacher education literature, is that reflective thinking is a "crucial process for teacher professional growth" (Sprinthall, Reiman, & Thies-Sprinthall, 1996, p. 688). Educators have moved beyond the debate regarding the merits of reflection to using professional development approaches that actually engage educators in reflection. You can become engaged in the process of reflective behavior by participating in action research, professional writing, study groups, curriculum development and analysis, and the development of professional portfolios. Fostering critical inquiry into professional practice develops a greater understanding of teaching and learning. Throughout the processes of critical inquiry or of maintaining a portfolio, you may develop a greater capacity to solve problems and to assume responsibility for professional decisions.

The reflection process is pivotal in developing a professional portfolio. As Burke suggests, "Without written commentaries, explanations, and reflections, the portfolio is no more than a notebook of artifacts or a scrapbook of teaching mementos. Such a portfolio does not reveal the criteria for collecting the contents, the thoughts of why the items were selected, or what the teacher and the students learned" (1997, p. 90). The reflective aspect of portfolios takes learning to a deeper level of understanding. The metacognition that occurs when you examine why a situation was meaningful, or consider alternative strategies for solving a problem, allows you to develop valuable insights about your professional work. When you think about how you learn, you can seek generalizations, tease out essential learnings, and apply them to new circumstances and diverse situations. The process of writing what you are thinking can illuminate and clarify your understanding of experiences. If you then share your written reflections, you increase the likelihood of attaining new levels of understanding or clarification. As Burke states, "The more practitioners take the time to reflect on their own experiences, the more they will begin to make the connections between prior knowledge, current learnings, and future applications" (1997, p. 97). Making such connections is the purpose for including reflections in the portfolio process.

There are many ways to incorporate reflection and metacognitive strategies into your portfolio. Using a range of reflective approaches can help maintain your interest and motivation throughout the process. The following reflection tools and techniques can help you explore and develop your professional thinking. The following reflective approaches demonstrate a variety of reflection techniques. The final technique, Reflective Summary, is accompanied by a sample reflection.

PMI: Starting with a work or learning sample from your portfolio (e.g., study group log sheet, videotaped lesson, professional development growth plan, conference notes), outline your reflection on the experience by using a graphic organizer. The PMI format (see **Appendix P**) encourages you to consider different perspectives of that experience: P = Plus; M = Minus; I = Interesting.

Reflection Sheet: The reflection sheet is a commentary sheet attached to the learning sample. It often lists a set of questions that summarize key learnings: What is your entry about? Why did you choose this entry?. The reflection sheet can be a common framework for all reflections in your portfolio (see **Appendix Q**).

Stems: Prompts that trigger responses are stems (see **Appendix R**). Your response to the prompt often provides insight into what you are thinking and why a work or learning sample is meaningful to you. It is common for one stem to be used for each portfolio sample, but combinations are also possible. Select stems that are appropriate for your needs.

Reflective Summary: A final reflection can be a powerful entry in the portfolio because it synthesizes experiences and learning. Use the steps and sample reflective summary in **Activity 19** as a guide.

Storing and Organizing Your Portfolio

Although your initial storage for work and learning samples may be a file cabinet drawer, box, or empty cabinet space, selecting a special organizer creates an important psychological beginning to the portfolio process. Have fun finding a storage container—go to a few stores or hunt around your home to find a special storage place for your samples. Using a specific container (with a finite size) encourages you to be selective in collecting samples. In addition, you can cull entries from the container to create a best work portfolio for job interviews. Showcase your best work in a plastic pocket folder, accordion case, decorated photo album, or looseleaf binder. In deciding what container to use for showcase purposes, consider advantages and disadvantages. For example, a

computer disk is compact, but the disk may not be compatible with whatever is available at the viewing site.

In addition to decisions about storage, you'll make decisions about how to organize the entries. Your audience requires an explanation of and a guide to your portfolio's organization. The following items may assist your audience in understanding how you have constructed your particular collection of entries:

Working Table of Contents or Tracking Form. A working table of contents is a useful way to organize the portfolio while it is being developed. It is usually chronological with each entry titled and dated as it is placed in the portfolio. A working table of contents or tracking form often enables the viewer to have a snapshot of the process, including the timing of entries, a list of who has responded to those entries, and the categories and outcomes or goals targeted. It also helps you to find and create patterns in your work and to determine what goals might emerge from those patterns.

Final Table of Contents. After compiling a showcase portfolio, add a polished table of contents. The table of contents provides a framework for the viewer and is a convenient reference for you and others in conference and interview situations.

Letter of Introduction. A letter of introduction that welcomes others into the portfolio serves as a critical point of orientation. The letter gives you the chance to tell your audience about your portfolio. This type of introduction may explain the focus or purpose of the portfolio, the time frame involved, the targeted goals, and other key elements. It may also highlight what the process has meant to you. An introductory letter is usually the last piece written for a portfolio and is a significant tool for sharing your learning with others.

As you prepare your portfolio, this self-portrait, give thought and consideration to creativity and

ACTIVITY 19
Reflective Summary

Use this activity and sample response to help you get started with your own reflective process.

• Select five entries that profile your professional development and your developing philosophy of education over the course of the last year.

• Do a one-page reflective summary explaining your rationale for the five entries selected. Your rationale should include specific examples from the entries that demonstrate growth in thought or action. (Be prepared to use the evidence from these five entries to engage in a professional interview.)

A Teacher's Reflective Summary

The following is a reflective summary based on the procedure outlined above. The summary was written by a preservice teacher at the Ontario Institute for Studies in Education of the University of Toronto in her second year of a two-year teacher education program. The summary is based on five artifacts she selected from her portfolio.

Name: Melanie, March 21
Purpose: A synthesis of my professional performance and emerging philosophy of education over the course of Year Two.

If Year One was spent building the theoretical foundations of teaching, then it can be said that Year Two was spent expanding on those foundations. The opportunities that I had to develop what I had learned in Year One, to hone my craft so to speak, were invaluable to my continuing growth. These opportunities strengthened what I believe is important to the teaching profession and allowed me to develop deeper insights into what it means to belong to a community of learners.

I would have to say that collaboration is a significant cornerstone of learning in Year Two.

My entry, "Collaborative Inquiry Conference," exemplifies how much I value collaboration in all areas of learning, both within the school and within the larger community. By presenting findings from my collaborative action research at a conference, I was able to contribute some interesting insights about the role of small group discussion in science to other educators. I perceive collaboration as necessary, even vital, to the health of our profession. We cannot possibly expect to strive for excellence when we don't have the means in place to tap into each other's knowledge base and repertoire of experience. By engaging in activities that are collaborative in nature, we are promoting a model of learning that will not only contribute to the well-being of our students but to that society as a whole. My

experiences with collaboration have been rewarding and personally enriching. I will continue to foster a collaborative attitude in the belief that a community of learners that collaborates together is one that stays together.

My growth in Year Two was facilitated by my inquiry into the nature of change—what is change and how can it be effectively implemented? The entry on "Debates in Education" asks some critical questions about the discussions at the center of education. It is our responsibility, as teachers wishing to effect change, to be informed of the issues and to consciously shape their development. There is too much at stake for it to be otherwise. An experience on a school improvement committee this year provided an understanding of the many levels at which change operates. It takes skill and knowledge of the change process to be able to reach the desired outcomes.

As a result of my two internships, I have been exposed to the many legal and ethical principles by which a school is organized. I have a greater awareness of my obligations vis-à-vis the profession. The entry on "Allegations" derives valuable lessons from an unfortunate incident at my son's school. I realize that teachers are the recipients of much public scrutiny (and so they should be) and that we must, therefore, be very conscientious of the legal responsibilities of teaching and how they influence our actions.

"Targeting Social Skills" is about the importance of teaching social skills in order for students to experience optimal learning. Students need to take responsibility for reaching their goals and this can be achieved by using a

simple rubric to help them identify the criteria by which they are being assessed. The use of self-assessment attests to my belief that students are more focused on self-improvement when they have some stake in the assessment process. This promotes ownership of learning and reinforces the necessary skills for goal setting. As well, it allows students the opportunity to address their own learning needs, critical to the development of lifelong learning.

Finally, "The Meaning of Expertise—Initial Impressions" reflects my emerging philosophy on what we can do, as teachers, to inspire our students to go beyond normal learning. What do we mean when we call someone an expert and how can we instill the value of expert-like learning in the classroom? These questions tie in nicely with the whole concept of change insofar as effective change calls for a certain openness to challenge and creative problem solving. What better way to face the challenges in education than by ensuring that teachers and students have the necessary skills and knowledge to adapt and be resilient yet resourceful in times of flux? I see this as indispensable to the cultivation and preservation of a community of learning.

The themes or strands of learning I have highlighted in this cover letter provide the building blocks for further growth. By choosing them as my rationale for the five entries I've selected, I am hoping to have identified some significant images that have helped me become a lifelong learner who believes strongly in the value of theory in guiding practice.

individuality. The portfolio's format, cover, organization, and visual appeal offer viewers insight into you and your abilities. Although visual appeal is no substitute for educational integrity, rigor, and soundness, it does influence the audience's perception of the portfolio. Tasteful use of computer graphics, artwork, photographs, and icons adds genuine flair to your portfolio.

SHARING THE LEARNING

Sharing the learning helps to ensure that the portfolio process is a personal endeavor and a collaborative experience. According to Burke (1997), "It is critical that educators collaborate throughout the entire process. Selecting goals, planning implementation, and reflecting on successes and failures is much more meaningful when it involves more than one person" (p. 65). The feedback of colleagues, peers, mentors, administrators, supervisors, and potential employers enhances the depth of learning that can occur through the use of portfolios.

As you share your learning with a variety of audiences, you'll benefit from many new and continuing conversations about learning. As a professional, it is natural to want to communicate effectively with communities beyond a single classroom and school. Conversation can provide valuable feedback to you as a learner and can assist you in articulating and reflecting on learning and professional practices. By sharing ideas both orally and in writing, you'll gain different perspectives on your personal growth that will help you set new goals. Celebrating successes and assessing growth are often incentives for identifying next steps.

One way to share learning is to ask colleagues for feedback, which may help you select appropriate learning samples. Through coaching, questioning, and providing feedback, others can participate in brainstorming and clarifying ideas

for portfolio items. You may want to use some of the ideas for portfolio work and learning samples noted earlier in this chapter (see **Activity 18**, p. 118) as a starting point for your discussion with others.

When you share your learning with others, formally or informally, you are creating opportunities for additional reflection. Sharing can take many forms, including oral and written peer responses to individual entries (see **Appendix S**), interviews or conferences about the portfolio or portions of it, summative evaluations of the complete portfolio, and public celebration of professional learning. If you are sharing your portfolio with others during a job interview, for example, you may choose to highlight items from your portfolio that target specific questions. Even if your portfolio entries are not shown during the interview, the process of having developed them synthesizes your thinking within a framework and enables you to effectively and articulately discuss your learning.

Sample questions may be used in interviews, conferences, and other interactive forums where you are sharing your portfolio. The following questions may spark reflection for sharing your learning:

• Which portfolio entry would you consider the most significant in terms of your learning and development as a teacher? Why?

• What area in your development as a teacher has experienced the most growth? How does your portfolio support this?

• In what way does your portfolio demonstrate you are a risk taker?

• Which of the six categories (see **Activity 18**, p. 118) is reflected most strongly in your portfolio? Explain.

• What are your goals for the future in relation to developing the six categories in your portfolio?

• What has your experience been with the practice of collaboration? Choose an entry that gives evidence of this experience.

• What entry demonstrates measures you have taken to strive for equity?

• Describe a situation in which you were faced with a professional moral, ethical, or legal dilemma. Explain how you resolved it.

• Which entries best reflect classroom practices that you would use next year? Why?

• What will your portfolio tell others about you as a lifelong learner and reflective practitioner?

• In what ways do your entries demonstrate a connection between theory and practice?

• How is diversity reflected in your portfolio?

• How has your personal philosophy changed or grown?

• What does your portfolio say about your philosophy of teaching? Choose 1–3 entries for evidence.

• If you had to choose only one entry to represent yourself in an interview, which would you choose? Why?

• What would you like your portfolio to say about you?

• What have you learned about the process as a result of having kept your own professional portfolio?

• What professional development goals have you set for yourself as a result of your experiences so far?

GOAL SETTING

Goals for professional portfolios can be individually determined or can be affected by external requirements. Additionally, goal setting may be influenced and enhanced by feedback. The most effective goals should be meaningful to you and specific enough to be challenging and attainable. Colleagues can help by asking questions that narrow your focus or broaden the scope of your initial thinking. In this way, peers can help you to articulate clear goals and to connect them to specific actions. Set goals and time frames that allow you to achieve success and experience growth in a reasonable length of time. For example, focus on goals that can be reached within one semester or one year. **Appendix T** contains sample questions that may help you define your professional goals, especially short-term goals.

SELF-EVALUATION

Whether your portfolio is self-initiated or required by the school or another organization, self-evaluation is key to ownership of learning and the continuous improvement of professional practice. In particular, positive self-evaluation can encourage you to set higher goals and to continue to devote personal effort toward achieving those goals. The practice of self-evaluation can increase your professional self-confidence over time (Rolheiser, 1996).

Portfolios may contain a summary reflection that includes self-evaluation of the portfolio. A summary reflection should review your goals, highlight the entries that show evidence of the targeted criteria, and identify how you grew as a result of the process. Future goals may also be articulated. Writing a self-evaluation often serves to synthesize your learning and to celebrate your successes. Self-evaluation may, in fact, become a significant part of an introductory letter for the portfolio. The following are sample prompts to help you do a self-evaluation:

• Did I achieve my goals? Why or why not?

• What did I learn or how did I grow?

• What did I find out about myself as a learner?

• What did I find most challenging about the portfolio process?

• What was the most rewarding aspect of the portfolio process?

• What are my accomplishments to this point?

• What goals do I have for the future?

• What specific actions do I want to take in the future?

A professional portfolio is a portrait of you as a professional. Depending on your purpose for the portfolio, you can choose to target different goals and to express your growth, accomplishments, and goals in unique ways. Use your portfolio and the portfolio process as an opportunity for reflecting upon your growth as an educator and your progress in achieving formal or informal goals. If the purpose of the portfolio is to meet the requirements of your professional setting or to advance your career, the process of maintaining a portfolio still offers many opportunities for making decisions and achieving growth. Selecting samples that directly target requirements and identified categories offer valuable opportunities for growth and self-expression. The portfolio process should be an interactive one, where the ongoing sharing with others provides a powerful impetus for continuing cycles of reflection and learning. Use the framework outline in **Planner J** to assist you in making decisions about your professional portfolio.

A FRAMEWORK FOR MY PROFESSIONAL PORTFOLIO

Use the form below to assist you in creating or maintaining your professional portfolio.

1. The purpose of my portfolio is to _____
_____
_____

2. The type of professional portfolio I will maintain is ____ growth or ____ best work.

3. Entry categories I will use:

• _____
• _____
• _____
• _____
• _____

4. Referring to **Activity 18** (p. 118), what samples have I collected or would like to collect?

_____
_____
_____
_____
_____
_____

5. What tools and techniques will I use for recording reflections?
   ☐ PMI
   ☐ Reflection Sheets
   ☐ Stems
   ☐ Reflective Summary
   ☐ _____

6. How will I store samples and entries?

_____
_____
_____

7. How will I keep track of entries on an ongoing basis?

_____
_____
_____

8. What audiences will I have for entries and the portfolio as a whole?

_____
_____
_____

9. How will I share my portfolio with others?

_____
_____
_____

10. What specific goals have I identified for my portfolio?

_____
_____
_____

11. How will I formally incorporate self-evaluation into the portfolio process?

_____
_____
_____

12. How will I begin to learn more about professional portfolios? (See pp. 113–114 for ideas)

_____
_____
_____

AFTERWORD

We are educators with very different experiences: a university professor, a high school teacher, and a consultant. Our work is in different contexts with different learners, yet we share something important: a passionate belief in the power of portfolios. We began experimenting with portfolios in very different ways, reflecting the uniqueness of our work lives and the array of choices available to us. We share our beginnings with you, confident that *The Portfolio Organizer* will support you in your own decisions for success.

CAROL REMEMBERS

In 1989 I was at a retreat for the Faculty of Education, University of Toronto. At the end of a long day a small group of diverse colleagues are engaged in intense conversation. The topic? Assessment and evaluation in our university classes. What do they look like? What do we want them to be? We explored the fit between teaching excellence and assessment. My colleagues, like me, were grounded in the belief that teaching is about developing relationships and creating opportunities for collaboration. We discussed the alignment of our assessment practices to those beliefs. One group member offers to share some ideas on portfolios. We respond to those ideas enthusiastically, and we make a commitment to explore portfolios for a few months—to read and discuss relevant literature, to debate ideas, raise questions, reflect on our practices, and ultimately try portfolios in our classes as tools for instruction and assessment.

Little did I know that this one innovation would powerfully affect my teaching and my students' learning. Learning has occurred for every member of our team, as we supported each other through a variety of implementation dips. Learning has also occurred for my students, as they have endeavored to take ownership for their growth and to feel confident in directing its path.

Through the years my students have gone from experiencing portfolios with me in one class in their program to using portfolios as a synthesizing tool across all courses and fieldwork in their preservice program. What remains constant is each group's enthusiasm for and commitment to portfolios. I am encouraged by annual program feedback; the one item that is wholeheartedly endorsed by my students is the use of portfolios. With that endorsement, we continue to explore the process together.

BARB REMEMBERS

In summer 1992 I attended a workshop and learned about portfolio assessment. After being an English and Special Education teacher, I was teaching mathematics. As much as I enjoyed this change, I found that I was not "connecting" with students as I had in previous years. I missed discussing themes and ideas in stories and novels, and I particularly missed the richness of students' writing. The math anxiety that I was encountering in relatively competent learners was unexpected and I was struggling with finding ways to help students.

Portfolios sounded interesting, I thought, because they offer a lot of possibilities for communication. With this in mind, I decided to try them out with a 9th grade math class in fall 1992. Had anyone told me then that I was embarking on a path that would involve such significant shifts in my beliefs and practices, I never would have believed it.

My first set of students' portfolios were, quite simply, astounding. Never before had I experienced such comprehensive portraits of my students. Portfolios allowed me, then and now, to know my students as individuals. Students' thoughts, fears, and pride are communicated to me in ongoing ways, and their learning and effort are evident. Using portfolios has forced me to change and update many facets of my teaching, including multiple intelligences (how can I bring them into math class?), cooperative learning (well, if students are going to respond to their peers' work, I'd better help classmates develop trust and appropriate skills), and student self-evaluation (this is a partnership—the students' opinions about their work are vital to that partnership). Ultimately, an experiment that I tried with one class has grown to become something much more, because portfolios were, and continue to be, the single most exciting thing that I have ever done in teaching.

LAURIE REMEMBERS

The title of an article caught my eye, "Literacy Portfolios: Helping Students Know Themselves." It appeared in the issue of *Educational Leadership* (May 1992) on performance assessment. I quickly focused on the highlighted reflections of a 4th grade student who attended an inner-city elementary school. He was explaining to his teacher the significance of each item he had selected for his literacy portfolio. Accompanying reflections focused on samples of academic work and on personal items, such as photographs of family members.

Two immediate impressions struck me. First was the growth and accomplishment that the child conveyed, despite challenging circumstances. Second was the idea that a portfolio, as a student-centered assessment tool focused on student self-evaluation, could enable the realization of many educational goals and objectives. Those goals included developing a love of learning, becoming self-directed, achieving full potential, thinking critically, making reasoned judgments, and valuing collaboration. So my journey with portfolio assessment began.

My first step was to link the portfolio process with cooperative learning to create the type of supportive, trusting, and safe context necessary for sharing reflections. I saw the potential that the marriage of cooperative learning and portfolio assessment held for promoting interaction not only between teacher and students, but also among all students. Ultimately, in a supportive context, each student's confidence as a learner can grow. As one elementary student told me several years ago, "When you open your portfolio, you say, wow! Look what I did in September and how I have improved. It is amazing! My portfolio helps me try to do my work harder. I feel good about my portfolio and I like sharing it with others because it shows what I can do." And that is the whole point.

As these reflections reveal, we are teachers. Our pride in our profession is balanced with humility, as teaching is a calling of immense challenge and complexity. At the heart of our work is a strong belief that good teaching is about relationships. It is about relationships with the learners we teach, the subjects we teach, and the contexts in which we teach. As teachers, we want to create communities where relationships develop and where all participants continuously learn and grow. After 10 years, we believe that portfolios are a critical component of these learning communities.

APPENDIX A

BEST IDEAS FOR LEARNING SAMPLES

Use this template to record your best ideas for the kinds of learning samples your students may create (see **Activity 5**, p. 28).

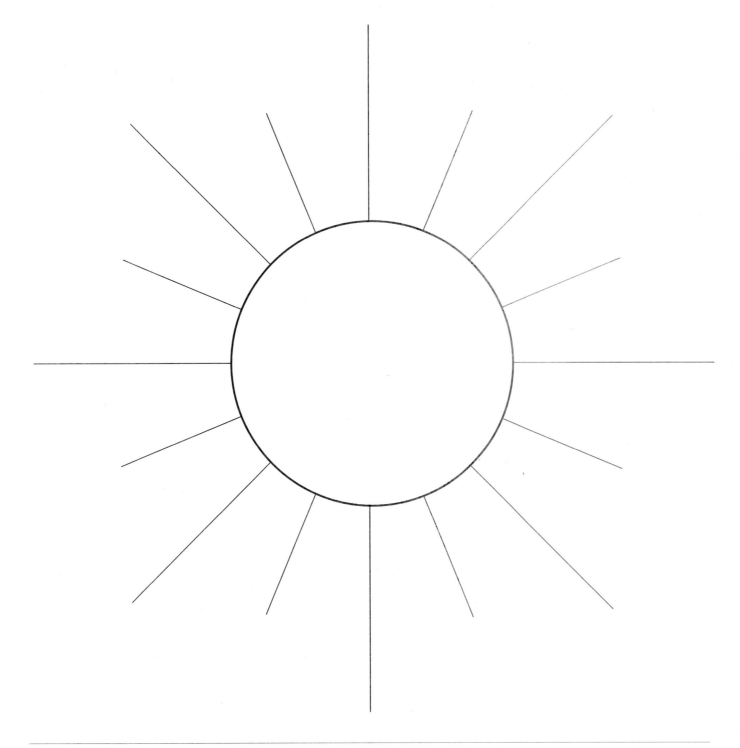

APPENDIX B

PMI AND ATTRIBUTES OF REFLECTION

Use a PMI chart to analyze the effectiveness of a student's reflection. List the things the student reflected on in the plus column, those things that should have been covered in the minus column, and things that are out of the ordinary or interesting in the final column. See **Figure 5.5** for a sample of a complete PMI chart.

PLUS, MINUS, AND INTERESTING (PMI) CHART

Student Sample	Plus	Minus	Interesting
Sample 1			
Sample 2			

ATTRIBUTES RECORDING CHART

What attributes are typical of a high-quality student reflection? Record your ideas.

Based on your analysis of student samples (**Appendix C**), what attributes best portray high-quality reflection?
1.
2.
3.
4.
5.
6.

APPENDIX C

STUDENT REFLECTION SAMPLES

The following samples of student reflections can be used to work through **Activity 6**. We have preserved grammar and spelling.

STUDENT REFLECTION SAMPLE 1

SARAH, GRADE 2

This is a fall seen and it has trees and mountins in it. The leafs are falling of the trees. This piece is special to me because I worked hard on it and it makes me feel good and calm. I feel proud about my work because I worked hard on it and I tryed my best. I learned that if you blened in the colours in the picture it looks nice.

STUDENT REFLECTION SAMPLE 2

NABEEL, GRADE 7

This entry is about my New France project. I chose this as an entry because I think that I learned a lot from it. I learned a lot about "Les Filles du Roi" and New France in general. It was an interesting project that I did well on. I feel that I also did very well in the actual museum presentation. I think I could've improved a little by adding a little more color to my display. That would have given it a lot more visual appeal. But I think I did very well, and this entry deserved to go in my portfolio.

STUDENT REFLECTION SAMPLE 3

MIKE, GRADE 6

This entry is about a debate of which CPU is better or most used: PC or Mac. I chose this entry because one of my best friends loves the Mac and I loved the PC. I learned that PC rules!

STUDENT REFLECTION SAMPLE 4

SARAH, GRADE 8

This entry is on the story that we had to do by looking at a picture. I like this entry because it involved a lot of my time and also because I had to flip around and look at the picture very closely to find out about what kind of story I'm going to write. The characters in the picture helped me a lot to make up the characters in my story.

I have learned a very valuable lesson from writing this story, to always check my spellings and grammar twice before I hand the story in. Because of this mistake I always lose a few marks.

STUDENT REFLECTION SAMPLE 5
JENNIFER, GRADE 10

This is the quiz that has been my worst mark out of all my marks this year, not just in math but out of all my subjects. I am disappointed with this mark but I am glad that we had the quiz because it showed me exactly what not to do on the unit test. This quiz was a great way to see how I could improve for my test.

The next time we have a quiz I would definitely like to get a better mark. I'm going to try and do that by checking all my answers after I have done the test and not rushing to get finished. Also, before the quiz begins I will look over my notes as a quick review.

STUDENT REFLECTION SAMPLE 6
CHRIS, GRADE 11

This (musical) piece is in the Lydian mode, thus has a different feel to it; there is a floating mood to it. This piece was my first attempt at writing in a Latin style; I find myself extremely attached to it as a result of this song's success. The difficulty in this song is in where the (root) chord is. It is easy to fall into the Fifth chord because it is the key of the song and the foundation of the mode. So, emphasis needs to be placed on the #11 (Lydian) chord as the root or Tonic chord. I learned simplicity is the key to writing melodies. Keeping with chord tones and staying with one main idea per section is essential.

APPENDIX D

TEMPLATE FOR INTRODUCTORY LETTER

The following is a template you can offer students to start their portfolio introductory letters. See **Figure 6.2** for a completed sample letter from Sarah, a 6th grader.

AN INTRODUCTION TO MY PORTFOLIO

Date: _____.   I am in ____ grade at _____.

My name is _____.   My teacher's name is _____.

- My portfolio is organized

- My portfolio shows I am

- My best piece of work is

- My favorite piece of work is

- The piece that shows my best effort is

- I want you to notice

- I think I have grown

- Next year I plan to work on

Signature: _____

APPENDIX E

TEMPLATE FOR GUIDING PEER RESPONSE TO PORTFOLIO ENTRIES

The following template can be used by students to respond to their peers' portfolio entries. Students may select from the sample starters below or create their own. See **Figure 7.1** for a sample of a complete peer response.

Name: _____.   I am reviewing the portfolio of _____.

Today's Date: _____.   The portfolio entry I am reviewing is called _____.

PEER RESPONSE STARTERS

- I like . . .
- You have shown that you understand . . .
- Something that captured my attention . . .
- I want to know more about . . .
- Key words for me were . . .
- I particularly valued . . .
- A question raised in my mind is . . . (be positive in your inquiry)
- An idea that sparkled for me was . . .
- Something I identify with is . . .
- What I found especially meaningful was . . .
- Something you wrote that pushed my own thinking was . . .
- I learned that you . . . (something positive)
- Thank you for reminding me how important it is to . . .

APPENDIX F

PREPARING FOR MY STUDENT–PARENT–TEACHER CONFERENCE

Student: _____   Date of Interview: _____

Time of Interview: _____

Each interview will last 15 minutes. During our class meeting, list the agenda topics you need to cover during this conference. Once you have listed the topics, organize your conference using notes to ensure all topics are covered.

AGENDA TOPICS

Topics	Notes (with evidence of learning where applicable)
Welcome	• Introduce my parents to my teacher • Explain the concept of a portfolio to my parents
Share my most significant portfolio entries	• Pull out two or three significant entries and describe why these are important to me and what skills, knowledge, and attitudes they demonstrate.

To Do List

Before the conference, I need to accomplish the following tasks:

- Organize my portfolio

- Use sticky notes to remind me of important topics for each entry

-

-

-

-

-

-

-

-

-

(adapted with permission of D. Couperthwaite, 1996)

APPENDIX G

PEER OBSERVER'S CONFERENCE FEEDBACK FORM

During peer conferences focusing on portfolio presentation, peer observers can use this form to offer constructive feedback. Presenters may also use this form as a reminder of important presentation skills.

Name: _____   Date: _____

1. Voice

- tone

- pace

- inflection or emphases

- articulation and clarity

2. Interview Presence

- body language—smiling, appropriate gestures, eye contact

- posture

3. Interview Sequence

- beginning—welcoming, sets the tone

- ending—summarizes, leave an appropriate final image

Feedback provided by: _____

APPENDIX H

TIPS FOR SHARING PORTFOLIOS WITH PEERS

Use this form to support students as they begin to share portfolios with peers. The student presenter and the student observer work together to fill out the form.

HERE'S WHAT MY PARTNER LIKES ABOUT MY PORTFOLIO

My Name: _____

My Partner's Name: _____

These pictures show three things my partner likes about my portfolio.

1.

2.

3.

(adapted with permission from R. Farr and B. Tone, 1994)

APPENDIX I

SAMPLE FORMS FOR PARENT RESPONSE

At the end of a student-involved conference or an adult review of a portfolio, use one of these forms to evoke meaningful responses for your students.

PARENT PORTFOLIO REVIEW AND RESPONSE

For a sample of parent's response to this form, see **Figure 7.5**.

Name of Reviewer: _____

Date:_____

1. Please record two successes or sources of pride as you review your child's portfolio.

2. Please record one wish for your child's growth.

(adapted from *Together is Better* by Davies, Cameron, Politano, and Gregory, 1992)

PORTFOLIO REVIEW FORM

Name of Student: _____ Date: _____

Name of Reviewer: _____

Please indicate your evaluation by circling the appropriate number on each of the scales below. Space has been provided for comments about the student's work. Thank you for taking the time to provide the student with valuable feedback.

1. Neatness and Organization of Work:

10 9	8 7	6 5	4 3 2 1
Superior	Proficient	Adequate	Limited

Reasons:

2. Quality of Work:

10 9	8 7	6 5	4 3 2 1
Superior	Proficient	Adequate	Limited

Reasons:

3. Evidence of Effort:

10 9	8 7	6 5	4 3 2 1
Superior	Proficient	Adequate	Limited

Reasons:

4. Please indicate below which item in the portfolio impressed you the most, and give reasons for your choice:

TOTAL : /30

PARENT AND STUDENT PORTFOLIO REVIEW

Please take some time to have your child present the portfolio to you. Ask questions about it: What makes your child proud of it? What has been a challenge? Then take a moment to complete this form and discuss it with your son or daughter. Please remember to keep your comments positive and constructive—this should be a celebration of your child's accomplishments. If English is not your first language, you may choose to complete it in your native language. Your son or daughter can give a brief translation on the back.

1. As you review your child's portfolio, what makes you particularly proud of your child?

_____

_____

_____

_____

_____

2. In what areas do you see the greatest growth?

_____

_____

_____

_____

_____

3. What is the most important change you have seen in your son or daughter this year?

_____

_____

_____

_____

_____

_____   _____
Signature   Date

JOINT RESPONSE TO A PORTFOLIO ENTRY

Use this structured approach to have the student and an adult respond to the prompts given.

Student	Adult
1. I really like	
2. When I read this I felt . . . because . . .	
3. I would change . . . because . . .	

APPENDIX J

FOUR RESPONSES TO LEARNING

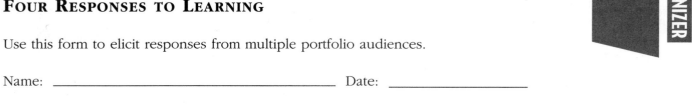

Use this form to elicit responses from multiple portfolio audiences.

Name: _____ Date: _____

Portfolio Entry Title: _____

Student's Comments	Parent's Comments
This entry is part of my portfolio because	Here's what I learned from looking at this entry

Peer's Comments	Teacher's Comments
I especially liked	This demonstrates that you have accomplished [particular criteria]

APPENDIX K

STUDENT'S GOAL SETTING SHEET

Use this form for students who need some structure in setting and reviewing goals. A sample of a student's response to this goal setting sheet is shown in **Figure 8.2**.

Name: _____ Date: _____

Area of Focus: _____

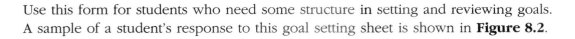

Strengths:

Challenges:

My Goal:

What will I do to achieve my goal?

-
-
-

Target date: _____

(adapted from Rolheiser, 1996, p. 94)

APPENDIX L

FORMS FOR SETTING GOALS

The following forms can help you provide your students with structure in the portfolio process. Adjust the ideas to fit the age and maturity levels of your students. Refer to Chapter 8 for suggestions on setting goals.

MY REPORT CARD ON SOCIAL SKILLS

Name: _____   Date: _____

	Student's Response		Teacher's Response	
	Yes	Needs Improvement	Yes	Needs Improvement
I wait politely				
I share with others				
I check for good listening				
I take turns				

(adapted from Rolheiser, 1996, p. 86)

USING PEER FEEDBACK TO SET GOALS

THE PORTFOLIO ORGANIZER

Name: _____ Date: _____

1. My peers noted the following strengths in my portfolio:

2. Here are the suggestions my peers made to improve my portfolio:

3. Based on the above feedback, here is a goal I want to reach:

4. Specific ways I can reach my goal:

COOPERATIVE GROUP WORK

Name: _____ Date: _____

1. Aspects of cooperative group work that are difficult for me:

2. Aspects of cooperative group work that are easy for me:

3. Goal for the future:

4. Actions I can take to help me reach my goal:

(adapted from Rolheiser, 1996, p. 97)

RECORDING GOALS AND ACTION PLANS

Name:

Subject and Grade:

Date of first review:

Academic Goal:

Work Habits Goal:

Action Plan: 1.

2.

3.

Date of second review:

Was the Academic Goal reached?   _____ Yes   _____ No

Why or why not?

Future Academic Goal:

Was the Work Habits Goal reached? _____ Yes   _____ No

Why or why not?

Future Work Habits Goal:

APPENDIX M

TEMPLATE FOR GENERIC RUBRICS

Use this template to draft your own rubric for portfolio evaluation. See **Figure 9.2** for a sample of a complete rubric.

Name: _____ Date: _____

Rated by: ☐ Self ☐ Peer _____ ☐ Teacher ☐ Other _____
                                    (name)   (name and relationship)

	1	2	3	4	5		

Criteria	Low	Middle	High
Score: _____			
Score: _____			
Score: _____			
Score: _____			

Comments:

Total Score: _____

(adapted from Rolheiser, 1996)

APPENDIX N

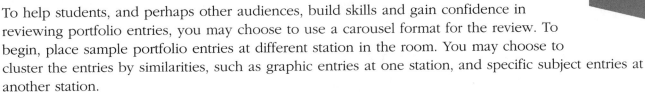

CAROUSEL RECORDING SHEET

To help students, and perhaps other audiences, build skills and gain confidence in reviewing portfolio entries, you may choose to use a carousel format for the review. To begin, place sample portfolio entries at different station in the room. You may choose to cluster the entries by similarities, such as graphic entries at one station, and specific subject entries at another station.

In small groups, the students rotate through the stations, examining the samples and recording comments either individually or as a small group. Sharing the observations and questions in a large group is a good closing exercise. This recording sheet is linked to Chapter 10, reviewing samples of student portfolios.

After exploring the material on display, here are some of my observations:

1.

2.

3.

4.

5.

Here are some of my questions:

1.

2.

3.

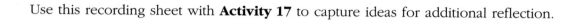

APPENDIX O

TIME CAPSULE RECORDING SHEET

Use this recording sheet with **Activity 17** to capture ideas for additional reflection.

This is me!

- Draw a picture of yourself or something important about you.

- List three things that tell who you are. The first item can be personal, followed by two professional things about yourself.

1. Personal _____

2. Professional_____

3. Professional_____

APPENDIX P

PMI REFLECTION

Name: _____ Date: _____

Identify the Work or Learning Sample:

List the attributes of the sample you are assessing in the appropriate column.

Plus	Minus	Interesting

APPENDIX Q

PORTFOLIO REFLECTION SHEET

Name: _____

Title of Entry: _____

Entry Date: _____

IDENTIFY THE PRIMARY CATEGORY FOCUS FOR THIS PORTFOLIO ENTRY.

Diversity	Curriculum, Instruction, and Assessment	Ethics and Legalities	Active Learner	Collaboration	Philosophy

DESCRIBE YOUR ENTRY.

Use the following prompts to begin the description of your entry.

- What is your entry about?
- Why did you choose this as an entry?
- What did you learn?
- How did you grow?

APPENDIX R

STEMS FOR REFLECTION

The following are some stems you can use for reflection.

☐   This was meaningful to me because . . .

☐   This entry demonstrates my understanding of . . .

☐   I am very proud of this entry because . . .

☐   I am not satisfied with this entry because . . .

☐   Something I would like others to notice about this entry . . .

☐   A question I want to pursue as a result of this entry . . .

☐   This entry shows evidence of my growth toward my goal because . . .

☐   This entry demonstrates a challenge because . . .

☐   I have gained insight as a result of this entry because . . .

☐   I would like to pursue additional learning in this area because . . .

APPENDIX S

COLLEAGUE'S RESPONSE TO A PROFESSIONAL PORTFOLIO

Ask a colleague to respond to your portfolio entries. You may offer your colleague guidance by offering the prompts in **Appendix E**.

Colleague's Signature: _____

Date of Sharing: _____

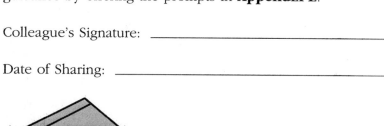

APPENDIX T

IDENTIFYING PROFESSIONAL GOALS

1. What general professional area or topic interests you? What area or topic would you be most interested in exploring?

2. Which key question intrigues you? What are some related questions?

3. If you were to choose to enhance an area of your own instructional practices, what would it be?

4. Based on the above questions what might be your identified goal?

5. What actions would you need to achieve your goal?

6. What evidence can show that you have achieved your goal?

LIST OF FIGURES

REFERENCES

Arends, R. I. (1991). *Learning to teach.* (2nd ed.). New York: McGraw-Hill.

Arends, R. I. (1994). *Learning to teach.* (3rd ed.). New York: McGraw-Hill.

Association for Supervision and Curriculum Development. (1992). *Redesigning Assessment: Portfolios.* [Videotape]. Alexandria, VA: ASCD.

Bandura, A. (1977). *Social learning theory.* Englewood Cliffs, NJ: Prentice-Hall.

Bellanca, J. (1992). *The cooperative think tank 2.* Palatine, IL: IRI/Skylight.

Bennett, B., Rolheiser, C., & Stevahn, L. (1991). *Cooperative learning: Where heart meets mind.* Toronto, Canada: Educational Connections.

Bower, B. (1994). *Portfolio assessment and evaluation.* Whitby, Canada: Durham Board of Education.

Brown, A. L. (1980). Metacognitive development and reading. In R. J. Spiro, B. C. Bruce, & W. F. Brewer (Eds.), *Theoretical issues in reading comprehension* (pp. 458–482). Hillsdale, NJ: Lawrence Erlbaum.

Brown, A. L. (1987). Metacognition, executive control, self-regulation, and other more mysterious mechanisms. In F. Weinert & R. Kluwe (Eds.), *Metacognition, motivation, and understanding* (pp. 65–116). Hillsdale, NJ: Lawrence Erlbaum.

Brubacher, M., & Payne, R. (1985). The team approach to small group learning. *Indirections* 8,(1–2), pp. 140-152.

Bruning, R. H., Schraw, G. J., & Ronning, R. R. (1995). *Cognitive psychology and instruction* (2nd ed.). Englewood Cliffs, NJ: Prentice-Hall.

Burke, K. (1997). *Designing professional portfolios for change.* Arlington Heights, IL: IRI Skylight.

Burke, K., Fogarty, R., & Belgrad, S. (1994). *The mindful school: The portfolio connection.* Palatine, IL: IRI/Skylight.

Campell, D. M., Cignetti, P. B., Melenyzer, B. J., Nettles, D. H., & Wyman, R.M., Jr. (1997). *How to develop a professional portfolio.* Needham Heights, MA: Allyn & Bacon.

Clemens, M. (1999, February). The Ontario curriculum exemplars project [Workshop]. In *Proceedings from communicating student learning: The third conference on assessing, testing and reporting achievement.* Toronto, Ontario, Canada: The Ontario Ministry of Education and Training and The Learning Consortium.

Conference Board of Canada, Corporate Council on Education. (1992). *Employability skills profile* [Pamphlet]. Ottawa, Ontario, Canada: The Conference Board of Canada.

Covey, S. (1989). *The seven habits of highly effective people: Powerful lessons in personal change.* New York: Simon & Schuster.

Danielson, C. (1997). *A collection of performance tasks and rubrics: Upper elementary school mathematics.* Larchmont, NY: Eye on Education.

Danielson, C., & Abrutyn, L. (1997). *An introduction to using portfolios in the classroom.* Alexandria, VA: ASCD.

Davies, A., Cameron, C., Politano, C. & Gregory, K. (1992). *Together is better: Collaborative assessment, evaluation and reporting.* Winnipeg, Manitoba, Canada: Peguis.

Delclos, V. R., & Harrington, C. (1991). Effects of strategy monitoring and proactive instruction on children's problem-solving performance. *Journal of Educational Psychology, 83*(1), 35–42.

Dillard, Annie. (1989). *The writing life.* New York: HarperCollins.

Educators in Connecticut's Pomperaug Regional School District 15. (1996). *A teacher's guide to performance-based learning and assessment.* Alexandria, VA: ASCD.

Farr, R. & Tone, B. (1994). *Portfolio and performance assessment.* Fort Worth, TX: Harcourt Brace & Co.

Fisher, C. J., Fox, D. L., & Paille, E. (1996). Teacher education research in the English language arts and reading. In J. Sikula (Ed.), *Handbook of research on teacher education* (2nd ed.). New York: Simon & Schuster Macmillan.

Fullan, M., & Stiegelbauer, S. (1991). *The new meaning of educational change* (2nd ed.). New York: Teachers College Press.

Fullan, M., Bennett, B., & Rolheiser-Bennett, C. (1990). Linking classroom and school improvement, *Educational Leadership, 47*(8), 13–15, 17–19.

Gardner, H. (1983). *Frames of mind: The theory of multiple intelligences.* New York: Basic Books.

Gardner, H. (1996). Are there additional intelligences? The case for naturalist, spiritual, and existential intelligences. In J. Cane (Ed.), *Education, Information, and Transformation.* Englewood Cliffs, NJ: Prentice-Hall.

Hargreaves, A., & Fullan, M. (1999). *What's worth fighting for out there?* New York: Teachers College Press.

Jacobs, J. E. & Paris, S. G. (1987). Children's metacognition about reading: Issues in definition, measurement, and instruction. *Educational Psychologist, 22,* 255–278.

Johnson, B. (1996). *The performance assessment handbook: Portfolios and Socratic seminars.* Princeton, NJ: Eye on Education.

Joyce, B., & Weil, M. (1996). *Models of teaching* (5th ed.). Needham Heights, MA: Allyn & Bacon.

Kagan, S. (1990). *Cooperative learning resources for teachers.* San Juan Capistrano, CA: Resources for Teachers.

Lazear, D. (1991). *Seven ways of knowing: Teaching for multiple intelligences.* Palatine, IL: Skylight Publishing.

Ontario College of Teachers (1999, March). Standards of practice for the teaching profession, *Professionally Speaking,* Toronto, Canada: Ontario College of Teachers.

Ontario Ministry of Education and Training. (1997). *The Ontario Curriculum, Grades 1–8: Language.* Toronto, Canada: Queen's Printer for Ontario.

Paulson, F. L., Paulson, P. R., & Meyer, C. A. (1991). What makes a portfolio a portfolio? *Educational Leadership, 48*(5), 60–63.

Random House Webster's Dictionary (3rd ed.).(1998). The Ballantine Publishing Group, division of Random House, Inc.: New York.

Rolheiser, C. (Ed.). (1996). *Self-evaluation: Helping students get better at it!* Toronto, Ontario, Canada: Ontario Institute for Studies in Education of the University of Toronto & The Durham Board of Education.

Rolheiser, C. (Ed.). (1996). *Self-evaluation . . . Helping students get better at it!* Ajax, Ontario, Canada: VisuTronX.

Rolheiser, C. (1998). *Visual tools for action research.* Unpublished manuscript.

Ross, J. A., Rolheiser, C., & Hogaboam-Gray, A. (1998). Skills training versus action research inservice: Impact on student attitudes to self-evaluation. *Teaching and teacher education, 14*(5), 463–477.

Ross, J. A., Rolheiser, C., & Hogaboam-Gray, A. (1999). Effects of collaborative action research on the knowledge of five Canadian teacher-researchers. *The Elementary School Journal, 99*(3), 255–274.

Ross, J.A., Rolheiser, C., & Hogaboam-Gray, A. (2000, January). Effects of self-evaluation on narrative writing. *Assessing Writing, 6*(1), 107–132.

Scherer, M. (1999). The understanding pathway: A conversation with Howard Gardner. *Educational Leadership, 57*(3), 12–16.

Schon, D. (1983). *The reflective practitioner.* New York: Basic Books.

Schon, D. (1987). *Educating the reflective practitioner.* San Francisco: Jossey-Bass.

Schwartz, S. & Bone, M. (1995). *Retelling, relating, reflecting: Beyond the 3 R's.* Concord, ON: Irwin.

Schwartz, S. (1996). Workshop notes.

Seely, A. (1996). *Portfolio assessment.* Melbourne, VI: Hawker-Brownlow Education.

Shaklee, B. D., Barbour, N. E., Ambrose, R., & Hansford, S. J. (1997). *Designing and using portfolios.* Needham Heights, MA: Allyn & Bacon.

Sprinthall, N. A., Reiman, A. J., & Thies-Sprinthall, L. (1996). Teacher professional development. In J. Sikula (Ed.). *Handbook of research on teacher education* (2nd ed.). New York: Simon & Schuster Macmillan.

Swanson, H. L. (1990). Influence of metacognitive knowledge and aptitude on problem solving. *Journal of Educational Psychology, (82)*2, 306–314.

Swartz, R. J. & Perkins, D. N. (1990). *Teaching thinking: Issues and approaches.* Pacific Grove, CA: Midwest.

INDEX

ABOUT THE AUTHORS

Carol Rolheiser is associate dean, Ontario Institute for Studies in Education of the University of Toronto (OISE/UT). She is a committed leader in school district and university partnerships, concentrating on teacher education reform, teacher development, school improvement, and managing educational change. Rolheiser's professional experience includes work as an elementary school teacher, district consultant, and school administrator. She has chosen a multidimensional scholarship path, but continues to be strongly based in cooperative learning, an area of research, development and teaching expertise. Rolheiser's work as a teacher, researcher, and international staff development consultant has emphasized instructional and assessment innovation, including portfolio assessment and student self-evaluation. Her work is reflected in a range of publications, including many journal articles and book chapters. She has coauthored an interactive resource book, *Cooperative Learning: Where Heart Meets Mind,* and edited *Self-Evaluation: Helping Students Get Better At It!*

Carol Rolheiser, OISE/University of Toronto, 252 Bloor St. West, Toronto, Ontario 5S 1V6, Canada. E-mail: crolheiser@oise.utoronto.ca

Barbara Bower teaches high school English and mathematics for The Durham District School Board in Ontario, Canada. She has been using portfolio assessment with students since 1992, and has facilitated conference and workshop sessions on portfolio assessment and student self-evaluation throughout Canada, especially in Ontario, and in the United States. Bower has written a handbook for teachers on portfolio assessment in mathematics, and has coauthored a resource document outlining cooperative learning lesson ideas for teachers of senior mathematics.

Barb Bower, e-mail: bbower@sympatico.ca

Laurie Stevahn is director of Professional Development Associates, an education consulting company providing staff development for effective instruction and quality learning. She is coauthor of *Cooperative Learning: Where Heart Meets Mind* and works with elementary, secondary, and university educators in designing and implementing a wide range of educational innovations including portfolio assessment and student self-evaluation, critical thinking and decision making, conflict resolution and human relations, organizational development and leadership for change.

Laurie Stevahn, e-mail: steva002@tc.umn.edu

RELATED RESOURCES: PORTFOLIOS

ASCD stock numbers are noted in parentheses.

Audiotapes

Assessing Children's Ways of Knowing: Portfolios that Tell a Story by E. Hebert
(#61292084)

Designing Performance-Based Assessment Using Dimensions of Learning by Jay McTighe
and Debra Pickering (#295194)

Easy Steps for Linking Portfolios to Standards by Teresa Navarro-Govelovich (#297099)

How Teachers Can Use Portfolios to Assess Thinking: Getting Started by Bena Kallick
(#294046)

Interdisciplinary Curriculum and Alternative Forms of Assessment by Bena Kallick
(#61293163)

Parent Involvement: More Power in the Portfolio Process by Donna Weldin and Sandra
Tumarkin (#297111)

*Performance Assessment and Instructional Change: The Effects of Portfolio Assessment on
Classroom Assignments* (#922192)

Portfolios: A Guide for Students and Teachers (#299219)

Portfolios for Self-Evaluation and Learning (#298284)

Portfolios: Linking Authentic Assessment with Instruction by J. Reynolds (#61292086)

Print Products

An Introduction to Using Portfolios in the Classroom by Charlotte Danielson and Leslye
Abrutyn (#197171)

A Teacher's Guide to Performance-Based Learning and Assessment by Educators in
Connecticut's Pomperaug Regional School District 15 (#196021)

ASCD Topic Pack—Student Portfolios (#197198)

ASCD Topic Pack—Teacher Evaluation/Teacher Portfolios (#197202)

Capturing the Wisdom of Practice: Professional Portfolios for Educators by Giselle Martin-
Kniep (#199254)

Improving Professional Performance [Special issue]. *Educational Leadership*, v. 53, n. 6
(#196007)

Videotapes

Redesigning Assessment Series (#614225)

For additional resources, visit us on the World Wide Web (http://www.ascd.org), send an
e-mail message to member@ascd.org, call the ASCD Service Center (1-800-933-ASCD or
703-578-9600, then press 2), send a fax to 703-575-5400, or write to Information Services,
ASCD, 1703 N. Beauregard St., Alexandria, VA 22311-1714 USA.